Scottish Rebuilt Buses

John Sinclair

© 2015 John Sinclair and Venture Publications Ltd
ISBN 9781905304684

All rights reserved. Except for normal review purposes no part of this book may be reproduced or utilised in any form by any means, electrical or mechanical, including photocopying, recording or by an information storage and retrieval system, without the prior written consent of
Venture Publications Ltd, Glossop, Derbyshire, SK13 8EH.

Dedicated to the memory of my friend Robert Grieves with whom I shared many happy journeys throughout Scotland, and who recorded so much of what took place during the time period of this book, both on film and in print.

Title page
In 1960, Laurie of Hamilton chose the Leyland body from a 1939 ex-Birmingham Corporation Leyland TD6 to replace the damaged Brush body on a newly acquired 1948 Leyland PD2 HD 7826. The hybrid vehicle subsequently passed to Central SMT in October 1961 remaining on front line service for a further four years. *(JS)*

Front Cover
In 1954, SMT replaced a damaged Duple body on one of its AEC Regents GSF 654 with a new Alexander style body from parts in its own coach works at Marine Gardens in Edinburgh. The resultant hybrid received a new registration number LWS 218 and a new chassis number SMT24. *(JS)*

Rear Cover upper
In 1950, Western SMT replaced the Alexander bodies on its Leyland TS8 specials with a contemporary version of the 39-seat body, and AAG 113 was still in use as a front-line coach at Dumfries depot where it was photographed in 1963. During the war, it was the Cumnock 'sleeper' for the 90-mile-long service from Dumfries to Glasgow. *(JS)*

Rear Cover lower
It was not uncommon to replace the utility bodies on Bedford OWBs with new Duple bodies after the war, and such a vehicle was WG 9918 new to Alexander in 1943 with an SMT B32F body to Duple design. The chassis alone was sold to Millburn Motors in August 1948, and Murray of Stranraer acquired it with this Duple C29F body. The possibility exists that this was a second-hand body, but there is no obvious source for it. It was photographed at their depot in April 1964 in a livery resembling that of Alexander, parked beside LVD 262, a 1955 Leyland Tiger Cub with an Alexander C41F body. *(JS)*

INTRODUCTION

The end of the second world war in 1945 signalled a difficult period for bus operators throughout the United Kingdom. Many had struggled on trying to maintain vehicles that were time expired. Replacement parts were in short supply. Skilled mechanics had been diverted to deal with military equipment. Routine maintenance had suffered and customary fleet replacement had all but come to a halt. The MOD had commandeered many vehicles, sometimes modern coaches, and many were not to return to their original owners. Some operators required additional vehicles urgently, particularly double-deckers, to transport staff and others to military establishments. Loadings on many services increased as fewer private cars were on the road, and some larger Scottish companies introduced programmes to convert single-deckers to double-deckers. The Ministry of War Transport allocated vehicles according to perceived need, but the 32-seat Bedford OWB was not a useful replacement for a full-size coach, and double-deckers were often allocated without regard to pre-existing chassis and body type.

Against this background, when the war ended, there was an urgent requirement for new buses. Coaches were also welcome, as many operators were anxious to restart private hire work, tours and provide premium vehicles for their express and long distance services. Large housing estates were beginning to appear at a distance from city centres, with few shops, public houses and opportunities for entertainment. Television was still a novelty and transport was required to take all ages into town centres to visit cinemas and dance halls. The MOD was beginning to release vehicles to a myriad of operators, but seemingly on a random basis. Some of the utility bodies were beginning to deteriorate already, particularly when unseasoned timber had been used, whereas the chassis were still sound. Some double-deckers with outside staircases were no longer acceptable to the public. Austerity bodies with wooden seats required refurbishment.

Faced with these challenges, most companies were keen to obtain new vehicles as soon as possible. Sometimes there was a mismatch between the production of a chassis and the availability of its body, and a suitable prewar body was reconditioned and used as a temporary measure. Often the temptation was to source new bodies for reliable prewar chassis such as Leyland Tigers and Titans, and AEC Regals and Regents, where replacement parts were readily available. Sometimes it was prudent to exchange bodies so that more durable chassis were paired with appropriate bodies. With an urgent need to modernise their coach fleet, particularly with the arrival of underfloor-engined vehicles, other operators would replace relatively modern bodies with the latest coach design, sometimes of a flamboyant nature. The bonus was that their original bodies could be used to prolong the life of other vehicles with sound chassis but deteriorating bodies. In some areas there was a continuing requirement for more double-deckers, and single-deck chassis, often relatively modern, were chosen. Their bodies in turn could be used to replace those older or indeed time expired.

The canny Scots have a tradition of 'mend and make do' with a psyche which favours the more conservative and economical policy of renovating older buses in order to get the best value from their existing fleet rather than splashing out on new machines. At the outset of the war, there were a number of small Scottish companies which built bus bodies and refurbished older buses, such as Croft, Pickering, Irvine and Campbell. In addition, there were smaller bus companies such as McLennan and Dodds who carried out major reconstructions in their own workshops. There had always been close cooperation between the larger companies, which formed the Scottish Bus Group, and the coachbuilding side of Walter Alexander which became a private company in 1947. This had existed since the early nineteen-thirties when relatively modern vehicles were often given new bodies, sometimes in the process converting normal control coaches to forward control. In the run-up to the war, this company started assembling bodies using Leyland components, and with the construction of the 'utility' double-deckers, a process sanctioned by the Ministry of War Transport, an innovative culture developed persisting after the war such that Scottish companies had a bodybuilder on hand to carry out widespread re-bodying to their requirements. In addition, the individual companies of what later became the Scottish Bus Group all had workshops capable of carrying out major bodywork activities, as indeed did the Corporations.

As in many parts of the United Kingdom, there was an increased demand for double-deckers during the war. Apart from the desire to avoid duplication wherever possible, they were often required for transportation to various military establishments, such as on the Solway coast and in Galloway. After the war, both Western SMT and SMT were anxious to restart their Anglo-Scottish services, and in the case of the former this was achieved by re-bodying thirty Leyland Lions acquired from various sources. SMT preferred to use new AEC Regals, but many of these were themselves soon rebodied, and used on the company's extensive network of tours and express services. At the opposite end of the spectrum, many of the rural services in Scotland were unremunerative and their continued existence was only justified by using elderly time-expired vehicles which had been refurbished and in some cases converted for OMO operation. While not on a par with the early thirties, the resulting variety of buses and coaches to be seen on the roads of Britain in the early postwar period was memorable. I was fortunate to be old enough to live through this period, and my interest in buses started when, in 1948 at the age of just seven, my mother put me on a bus (a Daimler CWA6 with a Duple body of Everingham Bros) for my unaccompanied daily seventeen mile journey to my school at Pocklington in Yorkshire. Unfortunately, it was to be 1956 before I took my first photograph and 1961 my first colour slide. Realising that I had still managed to catch the tail end of this colourful period, more for my own enjoyment I decided to see if I could capture the essence of this period of great transformation using some of my own slides. It is, however, glaringly not comprehensive, but just a representative selection showing some of the activities which took place throughout this period. However, this book could not have been written without the pictures from Robert Grieves unique and wonderful collection of photographs taken by himself, and those collected from the many individuals and bus operators throughout Scotland, with whom he developed a friendship throughout his lifetime.

ACKNOWLEDGEMENTS

The majority of the colour photographs have been reproduced from slides which I took during my travels around Scotland. These are supplemented by some taken by the late Robert Grieves as well as many B&W photos of his, or from his collection. I am grateful to Sadie Smart for her enthusiasm to see the work of Robert Grieves continue to appear in publications. Some more invaluable photographs from other sources are included. The full list of photographers appears below. If there are any photos that I have inadvertently not attributed correctly, I apologise in advance.

I would also express my thanks to Mark Senior and Ian Stubbs at Venture Publications for their work in designing this book, taking it from an idea through to the finished article. Mary and David Shaw are due my thanks for their diligent proof-reading, however, any errors are mine and not theirs.

John Sinclair
Milngavie
June 2015

PHOTO CREDITS

AC	AB Cross
JS	John Sinclair
RD	Ron Doig
RG	Robert Grieves / Robert Grieves Collection
RFM	RF Mack
RM	Roy Marshall
S	Surfleet

Of the twenty-six Daimler CVA6 chassis with Northern Counties L53R bodies ordered by Western SMT (BCS 428-53), the first four entered service in 1947 with second-hand, metal-framed Leyland bodies from a batch of ten TD4s (RN 7794-803) new to Ribble in 1936 and rebodied by Burlingham, which were obtained through the dealer Millburn Motors. A fifth (BCS 433) was diverted to subsidiary Greenock Motor Services and reregistered VS 4364, returning to WSMT in 1950 as KR 581. BCS 429 with a second-hand five bay-body believed to be Burlingham and fitted in Kilmarnock, the first of an intended five, was sold to Red and White Services entering service as GAX 332 with a Lydney body. These two were replaced by chassis with Northern Counties bodies, and BCS 453 appeared as BSD 453. A further five are believed to have been fitted with second-hand bodies, but never entered service as such. *(RG)*

The five Daimlers from the above batch (BCS 428/30/4/42 and VS 4364) with a further two (BAG 102/3) which also entered service with ex-Ribble Leyland bodies, were rebodied with Alexander H56R bodies in 1950, and continued to operate from Kilmarnock depot alongside the Northern Counties bodied vehicles, but because of their height, were confined to local services and those passing through one particular stance in the bus station. Both BCS 430 and 431 were withdrawn in 1963 and scrapped by Millburn Motors, with only five of the twenty-nine Daimlers seeing further service. BCS 431 had been fitted with the roof from a Northern Counties rebodied TD4 (CS 4500) in 1960 after an accident. *(JS)*

Alexander likewise fitted ex-Ribble bodies to three Leyland PD1s (fleet numbers RA1/2/5) thought to be by Roe, Eastern Coachworks and Burlingham respectively. RA1 entered service in July 1947 and RA2 in October, together with 6, the first of twenty-five PD1s (RA6-30) with Alexander bodies to the utility design. RA5 appeared three months later after being rebuilt in Falkirk like the others, and was allocated to Milngavie depot. First registered AWG 715, BMS 313/6 they became HMS 217-9 when fitted with new Alexander bodies in 1955. *(RG)*

Re-entering service in September 1955, now all based at Milngavie, they had an arduous life operating high frequency services to the large postwar housing schemes north of Glasgow, such as Drumchapel, and were delicensed in December 1966. RA5 saw no further service and all three eventually went to local dealers for scrap. RA1 and 2, however, came out of storage, both appearing in February at the newly-opened Cumbernauld depot which housed the former Carmichael fleet and 2, photographed outside the Milngavie depot, was not finally sold until a year later. *(JS)*

6

David MacBrayne, however, in 1947 used Park Royal C31F bodies fitted in 1936 to seven-year-old Maudslays to get into service the first two of its postwar fleet of 34 Maudslay Marathons. SB 3361/2, when new, had 20-seat bodies with mail compartments constructed by Vickers, but these were inadequate for the long distance service from Glasgow to Campbeltown, and when withdrawn, their Park Royal bodies passed to FGA 159 and FGB 418. Parked at Kinlochleven depot beside FGB 418 are two AEC Regals from a batch new in 1939 (CGE 203-6), also with Park Royal bodies, which make an interesting comparison. *(RG)*

FGB 418 and FGA 159 were eventually re-bodied by Duple in 1958 to provide more modern looking vehicles for its long distance services, and unusually completed 22 years' service in the MacBrayne fleet before sale to other operators. While FGA 159 was based at Ardrishaig depot operating services in Argyll, FGB 418 was allocated to Fort William depot, and is seen crossing Lochy Bridge on a local service in 1966, with the lower slopes of Ben Nevis in the background. After withdrawal, it saw a further two years' service with Garner of Bridge of Weir in Renfrewshire. *(JS)*

A more novel way of utilising existing bodies occurred in the Alexander fleet in 1961, when there was a need for high capacity double-deckers. Seventeen Leyland PD3s were created from parts taken from 7'6" wide PS1s with composite Alexander bodies already requiring renovation, and 17 of the batch of twenty 8ft wide OPS2s (fleet numbers PB1-20), fitted into new frames. The resultant vehicles (fleet numbers RB245-61) entered service with Alexander L67R bodies identical to previous batches of PD3s, except for exposed radiators. RB257-8 are shown parked here at Milngavie depot in 1973, incorporating parts from PB3 and 17 respectively. *(JS)*

PB3 was new in December 1951, and was allocated to Kirkcaldy depot for its entire life, passing to Alexander (Fife) with eight others in May 1961 after being converted to PS1 standard in 1960. The chassis were new in 1948 from a cancelled order by a New Zealand dealer, but their entry into service was delayed until a mere three months before the first of eighty-four Leyland Royal Tigers appeared. Initially kept for tours and private hires, it was latterly used on service work, despite retaining its coach characteristics. As such, it was painted into Fife's coach colours as seen here leaving the depot in 1964, but repainted into bus livery in 1966. It was withdrawn four years later, and sold for use in a contract fleet. *(JS)*

These hybrid Leyland PD3s ran for 15 years like previous batches, with eight initially being allocated to Milngavie depot, joined by RB261 in December 1975. Withdrawn six months later, it was photographed in March still in all day service, at the terminus of a local route, with our house visible in the background. Nevertheless, clearly belonging to another era and unsuitable for OMO operation, it was promptly sold to a local dealer for scrap. It had parts from PB18, an OPS2 from Dunfermline depot in Fife, which ended up with bus seats in red livery, and also sold for scrap in 1970. The three unmodified OPS2s (PB7/19/20) also ran in Fife, but were not regarded as in any way different. *(JS)*

The four Leyland OPS2 (PB2/6/10/1) which passed to Alexander (Northern) in 1961 were all repainted from Alexander's traditional blue and cream Bluebird livery straight into Northern's yellow and cream colours, but in service bus livery. PB11 (now classified as NPB11) is parked in the square at Turriff, an important Aberdeenshire agricultural centre. Photographed in 1968, it had recently been transferred from Aberdeen depot to the rural garage at Fyvie with an allocation of six buses, and although retaining its coach seats, was normally used on local and school runs. Withdrawn in April 1971, it ended up on a farm in Angus, but its sister PB10 is now preserved at Lathalmond museum. *(JS)*

Robert Tumilty, one of the members of AA Motor Services, an Ayrshire bus cooperative, used a more conventional route to convert one of his Daimler CVD6 single-deckers to a double-decker, using DAG 571, a Plaxton-bodied vehicle in his small 'Gailes Coaches' fleet. In a silver and light turquoise blue livery, it was new in 1950, and although operated from Tumilty's garage outside Irvine, it was not used on service work unlike four of the other five Daimlers in the coach fleet, which had Willowbrook bodies. *(RG)*

In May 1962, it reappeared with a new Northern Counties H35/28F body, having had its chassis widened to 8 feet. Now reregistered TCS 402, it retained its Daimler engine until replaced two years later by a Gardner 6LW out of XS 6751, an ex-Western SMT Daimler obtained for spares. However, after this major transformation, it had a short life of only nine years in service, before ending up with the dealer North of Sherburn in December 1971 for scrap. Pictured at the AA Bus Station in Ayr in January 1964, it is about to depart on the trunk route to Ardrossan, and was noticeable by virtue of its unique 'new look' style of radiator which was subsequently modified. *(JS)*

Western SMT's first new vehicles after the war were 49 AEC Regals with Burlingham B36F bodies, of which ten were for its subsidiary companies and registered accordingly. Only seventeen remained unaltered, 12 being converted to double-deckers in 1955, and 20 had their chassis extended to accommodate 38 seats between 1954 and 1957. The single-deckers were rebuilt to varying degrees, but all were withdrawn in 1959 and the double-deckers in 1963. BAG 107 was photographed early in its life at the terminus of a commuter route in to Glasgow. Delicensed in late 1953, it reappeared in 1955 as a double-decker, operating out of Carlisle depot, and ended up with a dealer in Rothwell. *(RG)*

The double-deck bodies were constructed at Irthlingborough by Bristol Bodyworks to ECW design, and four were allocated to Greenock depot for intensive local services, and eight to the former Caledonian territory which extended from Stranraer in the west to Carlisle in the east. BAG 74 was one of two based in Stranraer, and was photographed in 1962 outside the school at Newton Stewart awaiting its return to the fishing village of Port William where it was parked overnight. A year later it was sold, ending up with a contractor like three others of the batch, the remainder being scrapped. *(JS)*

Another Ayrshire cooperative, A1 Service, operated a high frequency service between Kilmarnock and Ardrossan. Member Andrew Hunter of Springside had two shares (fleet numbers 16 and 17) and in1950 purchased DCS 616, a Daimler CVD6 with a rare Irvine (of Salsburgh) 'Sun Saloon' C35F body which was replaced by a double-deck Massey body in 1958. Photographed at Ardrossan Bus Station in 1965 by which time a door had been fitted, it bore the fleet number 16A denoting a spare bus. Withdrawn in 1976, it was converted to open-top operating a circular tour in Stirling, and is now preserved. *(JS)*

In December 1966, Alexander (Northern) took over the long established firm of Simpson of Rosehearty, acquiring Leyland PS1s from the Yorkshire Traction fleet, which had been re-bodied as double-deckers by Roe. HHE 319-24 (NRA102-7) were new in 1947 with Weymann B32F bodies registered AHE 461/2/5-8. KHE 649/50 (NRA108/9) were new in 1948 to County Motors of Lepton with Roe B32F bodies, passing to Yorkshire Traction in 1956 and immediately re-bodied. In 1965, all eight double-deckers were acquired by Simpson. HHE 323 is seen here at Fraserburgh Bus Station waiting to return to Rosehearty. *(JS)*

The Simpson fleet of thirty-one vehicles was very varied, but the only other double-decker than those mentioned in the previous caption was HLW 144, new to LTE as RT157 with a Park Royal body, acquired in 1963 from Brown's Blue of Markfield. Although operated by Northern for two years, it was never painted into fleet colours, and sold to a dealer for scrap. Parked beside it at the depot in Rosehearty in February 1967 are HHE 320 and KHE 650 both with platform doors and still to be repainted, and examples of the highbridge body fitted to those rebuilt in 1955, and lowbridge version on the pair new to County Motors. These were both sold for scrap in October 1969. *(JS)*

The previous year Alexander Northern had acquired the twelve-vehicle fleet of Deeside operator Strachan of Ballater with seven Fodens, four AECs and a solitary Leyland PS1 HOM 776. This was new in February 1948 with a Santus C33F body to Stockland Garage of Birmingham, and re-bodied with this Duple C35F body in 1954. Acquired by Strachan in May 1960, it passed to Northern in May 1965, and was photographed after repainting into fleet colours in Aberdeen in July 1965. It operated from Aberdeen depot on rural services until transferred to the fishing village of Buckie in July 1969, being withdrawn in December, and ending up at Butlin's Camp at Pwllheli. *(JS)*

13

The urgent requirement for increased capacity during the war resulted in some Scottish operators removing modern bodies from Leyland and AEC single-deckers, and converting the chassis to take the 'austerity' metal-framed, double-deck body produced by Alexander based on pre-war Leyland designs. The conversion involved having the chassis stripped down, fitting new side frames and replacing the running units. Central SMT sent 28 TS7, one TS7T and one TS6 chassis to Stirling in 1944 and 1945 to receive their new bodies. TJ 3279 was a 1933 Leyland TS6 demonstrator with a metal-framed B32R body, seen here in the maroon and cream livery of Clydebank Motors, and acquired by CSMT in 1936. *(RG)*

TJ 3279 passed to Central SMT in June 1936 as T76 and was renumbered L209 when re-bodied in January 1945. Although numerically the last of the re-bodied batch, the Leyland TS7T VD 4459, which required altering from six-wheel to four-wheel, did not appear (as L205) until the end of the year. L209 was photographed near Waterloo Street Bus Station in Glasgow with evidence of body reconditioning with reglazed windows. Operating from Wishaw depot in the territory of the Lanarkshire Traction Company, a subsidiary of CSMT which was absorbed in 1949, it was sold in June 1959 for scrap. Western SMT similarly treated Leyland TS7 demonstrator TJ 6350. *(S)*

David Lawson of Kirkintilloch was taken over by Alexander in 1936 and the vehicles given fleet numbers in the Alexander series in 1938, but it remained a separate subsidiary with its red livery until 1961. The last new purchases before the takeover included a batch of six Leyland TS7s with locally built Martin C32F bodies for its 'Land Cruises'. SN 7135-40 with fleet numbers P449-454 were transferred to the parent company in 1943, converted to Leyland TD4 specification and re-bodied with new Alexander L53R bodies being renumbered R389/94/420/382/64/5. The original bodies were sold to the dealer Millburn Motors. *(RG)*

They were scattered throughout the Alexander empire, with SN 7136 later allocated to Inverness, passing to Highland Omnibuses in 1952. SN 7139/40 operated from the rural depot of Arbroath in Angus, finally moving to urban Milngavie in January 1960 for their final year of operation. Alexander converted 106 single-deckers to TD4 specification between February 1943 and April 1944 with fleet numbers R336-435/63-8, all being TS7s apart from a solitary Leyland LT6 chassis which had never been used. All were withdrawn by September 1961. Many of the original bodies saw further use, 21 passing to Western SMT, and others through Millburn Motors. *(RG)*

In 1935, 29 Leyland TS7s (CS 2001-29) with problematic metal-framed Leyland B32R bodies entered service with Western SMT (together with 20 TS7Ts) Of these, one was taken by the MOD, 23 were re-bodied by Alexander as double-deckers during the war and four as single-deckers in 1950. CS 2024, however, was converted to TD4 specification in 1950, and surprisingly appeared with a Burlingham H56R body, possibly as an experiment. It spent its entire life on local services in Ayr on the Doonfoot to Marchburn service, being withdrawn and scrapped in 1960, only a year after those re-bodied during the war. *(RG)*

The four single-deckers given new all-metal Alexander C35F bodies in 1950 (CS 2005/21/2/7) operated in Dumfries and Galloway remaining in service until 1963, and all saw further service with other operators. CS 2022 seen parked in the square at Newton Stewart in 1962 was allocated to the Stranraer area, and is waiting to take up its school run down to Whithorn where it is parked overnight. Sold by dealer Millburn Motors to a contractor in Salisbury, it was last licensed in 1966 when 31 years old. Most of the original bodies from those converted during the war were fitted to older TS1 and TS2 chassis. *(JS)*

Of the next batch of WSMT TS7s (CS 5227-71), 30 arrived in 1937 with Alexander C35F bodies, and 15 between 1937 and 1939 with Burlingham C32F bodies for the Glasgow to London service, all with full-fronts. The latter (CS 5227-41) were all re-bodied as double-deckers during the war, as were nine with Alexander bodies, two were burnt out in 1941, and nineteen acquired by the War Department in 1940. One of these was CS 5263 which was returned in 1943 and had lost its full-front by the time this photograph was taken. *(RG)*

Only three other TS7s with Alexander bodies were returned by the MOD, CS 5250/5 also in 1943 and 5269 not until August 1948. Consequently, when fleet numbers were allocated in 1948, it was given 21 which had been vacated by a Leyland LT5A just sold. All four were re-bodied by Alexander in 1950, with CS 5263 and 5269 running from Dumfries depot, seen here at the bus station on Whitesands still in coach livery. The other two were latterly allocated to Carlisle depot, all four being withdrawn in 1963. They were also sold to contractors, CS 5263 being based in Salisbury and CS 5269 in Southern Scotland. *(RG)*

17

The final batch of single-deckers before the war was of 25 Leyland TS8s (AAG 101-25) with 39-seat Alexander bodies, achieved by modifying the front end to allow the engine to protrude through the bulkhead. Five were immediately acquisitioned by the MOD, but one (AAG 121) was returned in March 1949 after being discovered locked in a shed on military premises. Given a contemporary fleet number 580, it returned to service with its original body until withdrawn in 1957. AAG 101 was delivered in a short-lived black and ivory livery, but is seen here after the war in red and cream with its usual driver and conductress on its regular service. Its radiator is spectacularly embellished with polished adornments. *(RG)*

The remaining 20 vehicles (AAG 101-16/20/3-5) with fleet numbers 162-81 were re-bodied by Alexander in 1950/1 with similar C39F bodies. Six (AAG 108-13) were allocated immediately to the Dumfries area in dual-purpose (cream and red) livery, and the remainder used on the Glasgow to Largs (via Renfrew) 'low road' service operated by Inchinnan depot. All eventually ended up at the various Dumfries area depots, and AAG 101/2 are parked here in April 1963, now in "bus' livery, at the already closed Whithorn station off their school runs from Newton Stewart High School. Withdrawn in 1964, they both ended up with contractors, 101 based in Belfast, and 102 in Glasgow. *(JS)*

Alexander had Leyland TS7s re-bodied in 1949, four (WG 4445/6/9/50) from a batch of ten (P331-40) new in 1937 with Alexander bodies. WG 4445/6 were new to subsidiary 'Simpsons and Forrester' of Dunfermline. All were allocated to subsidiary David Lawson with their new 30-seat bodies for their 'Land Cruises' and downgraded to service work in 1959. WG 4445 and 4450 were transferred to the small rural depot at Pitlochry in July 1961 where they operated the scenic service from Perth up the A9 to Pitlochry and Calvine for the next three years. WG 4445 was photographed at Perth Station in 1963, now in bus livery and showing 'Midland' ownership, and is now preserved. *(JS)*

When the Dundee area of Scottish Omnibuses passed to Alexander in December 1949, 55 Leyland single-deckers were transferred, including 17 TS7s with Alexander B35R bodies from the ASF 364-416 batch new in 1937. Two of these were converted to front entrance, but four (ASF 365/7/78/88) were re-bodied by Duple in 1951, the bodies having been ordered by Sutherland of Peterhead, recently taken over, for AEC Regal chassis. Reallocated to the Northern area, they were finally withdrawn in 1964. ASF 365, seen parked at Elgin depot in 1962, now preserved, was the last prewar single-decker in service with the Scottish Bus Group. *(JS)*

19

In 1950, 8ft wide Duple coach bodies were fitted to eleven of a batch of 50 Leyland TS7s new to Ribble in 1936, which extended their life with the company for a further ten years. They were sold to the Preston branch of Millburn Motors which had its headquarters in Glasgow, and RN 7765 was purchased by Loch Lomond-Loch Katrine Services who operated it from Stronachlachar to Inversnaid on the banks of Loch Lomond where it was photographed in 1965. This was an integral part of a Trossachs tour, which took passengers off the cruise boat on Loch Katrine, so that they could sail across Loch Lomond and return to Glasgow by road. *(JS)*

Millburn Motors played a key role in buying and selling buses throughout the West of Scotland, both fitting second-hand and new bodies to chassis for smaller operators. Such a bus was Leyland TS7c BWB 201, new to The Sheffield Joint Omnibus Committee C fleet owned by the railways, in 1935 with a Craven B32R body. It also was sold to the Preston branch of Millburn Motors, in January 1948, and had a new Duple C33F body fitted in the Glasgow premises, before sale to the small Lanarkshire operator Tennant of Forth, who operated schools and contract work. It was photographed at Lanark bus station in 1966. *(JS)*

Simpson of Rosehearty acquired three (OKP 988/90/3) of the shorter Leyland-Beadle rebuilds which entered service with Maidstone and District Motor Services (CO260/2/5) in 1952 with 26 coach seats. Having passed to the contract operator Sowerby of Gilsland in 1960, they moved north in 1962 as C31F and were used on a variety of work. OKP 990 was dismantled for spares in 1965 and 988 sold to a local contractor in 1966. OKP 993, however passed into Alexander ownership as P838 in December 1966. Photographed at Rosehearty, it was never painted into fleet livery, and sold for scrap two years later. *(JS)*

Another Scottish independent to acquire a Beadle rebuild from Maidstone and District, this time directly in 1961, was Mitchell of Luthermuir who operated a network of services in rural Angus, centred on a small village near Brechin. NKT 966 (CO238) new in 1951, was based on an AEC chassis, converted from C35F to B39F in 1954 and renumbered SO107. With a one piece blind, it was photographed in Brechin in 1965 beside KSC 555, a former Scottish Omnibuses AEC Regal IV with Alexander C38F body (B478) now with independent Alexander of Arbroath. Withdrawn in February 1967, it did not pass to Alexander (Northern) when Mitchell was taken over eight months later. *(JS)*

21

McLennan of Spittalfield who operated further south in Perthshire was an innovative company which constructed twenty-two new bodies and rebuilt many others. One of the more imaginative was their conversion of a Leyland TD7 into a single-decker. FOF 281 was new to Birmingham City Transport (1281) in 1939 with a Leyland body. Following bomb damage in 1941, it was fitted with a replacement top deck from a 1933 Morris Imperial with a Metro-Cammell body and reseated to H54R. Acquired in 1950 via the dealer Bird of Stratford-of-Avon, it was fitted with a platform door and ran until December 1953. *(RG)*

In June 1955, it reappeared after its chassis had been lengthened to thirty feet, fitted with a Leyland PD1 engine and a new 39-seat body. Reregistered GGS 688, it remained in service until 1968 when it was withdrawn and scrapped. It was photographed at Alyth in May 1965 on the 12.35pm service from Kirriemuir to Blairgowrie. By coincidence, the Bedford A3LZ FGS 817 waiting to leave on the tortuous route up to Glenisla also has a McLennan body. New to Gourlay of Alyth in 1954, it has a 20-seat body with a mail compartment, and would run for another four years. *(JS)*

22

McLennan converted one further vehicle in a similar manner. In 1948, Western SMT sold non standard ACS 929, an 'unfrozen' Leyland TD7 with a Northern Counties body, when only six years old. Withdrawn in 1950, it was rebuilt and appeared as EGS 914 three years later. Within two years it was sold to Niven of St Andrews, with whom there was often an exchange of vehicles, a small company which operated a town service and school runs. It was photographed there in July 1965, a month after withdrawal. Parked beside it is HFG 605, an Albion Victor with a Strachan body new to nearby operator Williamson of Gauldry. *(JS)*

A less complex conversion was of 18 Leyland TD4 chassis to TS7 specification in 1948, by extending the chassis frame and fitting new Burlingham C33F bodies. Western SMT was in urgent need of coaches at that time and acquired five, new to Glasgow Corporation in 1935 with Cowieson bodies (YS 2028/38/51/7/75), and 13 from Sheffield Corporation. The chassis conversion of YS 2057 was carried out by Millburn Motors, and it entered service at Inchinnan depot in May 1948, moving over to the Island of Bute in 1952 for its final five years, after which it was exported to Libya. *(RG)*

23

Another Glasgow Corporation double-decker to be converted to a single-decker was DGG 910, one of ten Guy Arabs (DGG 902-11) new in 1943 with Pickering H56R bodies. Acquired through dealer Gray of Braidwood, by Dodds of Troon, the largest of the three members of the Ayrshire cooperative AA Motor Services in 1951, it entered service in May 1953 with a new Roe B38C body. This was similar to a batch of twenty Guy Arab III single-deckers operated by Darlington Corporation, and after its chassis had been lengthened, DGG 910 was fitted with an Arab III style radiator. Withdrawn twelve years later, it was sold to a local contractor in Irvine. *(RG)*

An identical conversion was carried out on DVD 310, also a Guy Arab II, but new in 1948 with a rare Irvine of Salsburgh L27/28R body, one of only three double-deckers constructed by the Lanarkshire firm, who only built 24 bodies in total. This proved unsatisfactory, and Irvine sold it five years later to Dodds who scrapped the body and sent the chassis down to Leeds. It also reappeared in 1953 and was withdrawn in September 1965, being scrapped at their depot in Troon. It was photographed at Ayr bus station in 1963 waiting to depart on its journey up the Ayrshire coast to Irvine. *(JS)*

Another imaginative conversion of utility Guys to full length single-deckers took place at Marine Gardens, the coachbuilding department of Scottish Omnibuses. It had acquired 23 Guy Arabs new to London Transport, nineteen directly and two each from Highland Omnibuses and Alexander. Only eleven (E23-31) ran in service before, like the remainder, having their chassis overhauled, extending the wheelbase to 30' and fitting Gardner 5LW engines, before constructing new bodies to Alexander design. E24 (HGC 113) ex-LTE G334 with a Park Royal body is seen here in Glasgow on a local service to Clarkston. *(RG)*

The 23 single-deckers were given chassis numbers SMT1-23, and 13-17 became Scottish Omnibuses D1-5 (LSC91-5) which entered service at depots in the borders in 1954 and were withdrawn in 1962. Highland Omnibuses took the remainder, with the last six chassis (LSC 96-101) being fitted with 35 coach seats rather than 39, and LSC 101 was the last to be withdrawn in November 1966. These rugged vehicles operated throughout the Highland Omnibuses empire, and KSC919 is pictured here outside its dormitory at Helmsdale in August 1963 ready to take up the 8am service down to Dornoch. *(JS)*

Another 'new' bus created at Marine Gardens was SMT24 (LWS 218) which entered service back at Bathgate depot in July 1954 with an 8ft wide L53R body. Perhaps surprisingly, it had half drop windows. It remained there, employed on a wide variety of duties including works services to the local coal mines and an expanding BMC factory, until withdrawn in December 1966 when it was sold to a local dealer in Edinburgh. Photographed outside Bathgate depot in 1964, it had just been repainted from the light green livery into dark green colours, colloquially called Lothian green, and has retained the SMT diamond as fleetname. *(JS)*

LWS 218 started life as AEC Regent III GSF 654, new in November 1949 with an 8ft wide Duple L53R body, one of a batch of 20 (GSF 644-63) with fleet numbers BB61-80. In 1953 it was involved in a serious accident, after which its Duple body was scrapped, and a new body constructed. The remainder of this batch continued in service until 1966 without external signs of major rebuilding. GSF 645, photographed at Edinburgh bus station also in 1964, was coincidentally sold along with LWS 218 to the same dealer, Locke, in December 1966. It was, however, scrapped whereas the unique body of LWS 218 was later sighted near East Fortune hospital situated in rural East Lothian. *(JS)*

The body of LWS 218 appears to have been constructed using parts possibly obtained from the body shop of Alexander in Stirling. It even received a 'new' chassis number SMT24. The similarity to a batch of AEC Regents (BB21-60) delivered the previous year with 'post-austerity' Alexander bodies is quite striking, as shown in this photograph of the last of that batch (FFS 181) taken in Kirkcaldy in August 1965, still in the traditional light green livery. Surprisingly, for a bus that would be withdrawn only ten months later, it was being used on the premium service from Edinburgh to Kirkcaldy via the Forth Road Bridge. After sale, it operated in Northern Ireland with the contractor Cruden. *(JS)*

These Alexander-bodied Regent IIIs had a long life with Scottish Omnibuses, the first, BB21, which entered service in December 1947, being delicensed exactly twenty years later. It then saw further service with the contractor Smart in Tranent. BB41, seen here, was photographed in the high street in the industrial town of West Calder on a local service to Bathgate in July 1965 in Lothian green colours, but with Eastern Scottish fleetnames. It had been allocated to Bathgate depot since being transferred in 1958 from Airdrie depot which supplied vehicles for intensive services out of Glasgow. It was sold to the dealer Locke in 1968, but saw no further service. *(JS)*

27

Marine Gardens was busy renovating bodies for the newly formed Highland Omnibuses in 1952, but decided to construct a new body for one of a pair of Leyland TD3s (CK 4873/8) new to Ribble in 1934 with 6-bay English Electric Bodies and sold to Alexander in 1947. In 1952 they passed to Highland Omnibuses with the Inverness services of Alexander, and CK 4873 retained its body, albeit rebuilt in 1955. CK 4878, however, was sent to Edinburgh and reappeared in October with a 5-bay body, the front showing the features of SMT buses being overhauled at that time. The roof and rear dome, however, had the characteristics of the wartime Alexander bodies. Ironically, they were both withdrawn at the same time in 1957. *(RG)*

Western SMT also constructed a body from parts available in their body shop in Kilmarnock, producing a body similar to the pre-war Leyland design. ASD 253 was one of four Guy Arab IIs and four Daimler CWG5s delivered with Massey H56R bodies in 1943, all of which required extensive rebuilding using Alexander parts or re-bodying (ASD 94) by 1951. It was, however, unique, in that as a possible prototype project, the reconstruction was almost complete, using what appeared to be Leyland parts. It reappeared in May 1951 and ran for a further ten years, initially on the 76 mile trunk route from Glasgow to Stranraer. Photographed at Kilmarnock in 1961 when a Driver Training Vehicle, it was finally withdrawn in August 1964. *(JS)*

Another unique bus in the WSMT fleet was ASD 409, one of 15 Guy Arabs delivered during 1943/4 with Northern Counties L55R bodies. Delicensed in July 1948, it reappeared in December with what appeared to be a new body from Northern Counties. However, extensive research by Garry Ward would suggest that it was a warranty replacement but incorporating elements of the original body, such as the windscreen. Returning to Girvan depot, it remained on longer distance services until September 1961, when it was loaned to Highland Omnibuses for three months. After further use at Greenock, it passed to Northern Roadways, in whose livery it was photographed at Bridgeton Cross in September 1962. *(JS)*

Two other vehicles in this batch, however, ASD 404/5 received new ECW bodies in 1951. They then operated from Carlisle depot until March 1960, when moved to the other end of the country to Caithness, being acquired by Highland Omnibuses. Fitted with platform doors at Dumfries before transfer, they remained in Caithness until withdrawn in March 1965 and scrapped. Interestingly, ASD 406 and 408 with original Northern Counties bodies also passed to Highland Omnibuses, 406 also running in Caithness but withdrawn two years earlier. ASD 404 was photographed at Thurso depot in 1962, parked beside one of the rebuilt ex-London Transport Guys. *(JS)*

29

Another Western SMT bus with an Eastern Coachworks body to pass to Highland Omnibuses was Leyland PD2/20 GCS 232. New in 1955 with a Northern Counties L55R body, it was stolen from Clyde Street in Glasgow in October 1966 when operating from Newton Mearns depot, and crashed into a low bridge at Hurlford outside Kilmarnock. Having just received its five year COF, it was decided to fit the 1952 7ft 6in ECW body from previously re-bodied PD1 CCS 406 on to its 8ft wide chassis, and the Northern Counties body and PD1 chassis were scrapped. CCS 406 had been withdrawn prematurely in October 1966 for conversion to a tow wagon. *(JS)*

The resultant hybrid vehicle re-entered service in March 1967 at Newton Mearns depot, and was almost immediately transferred to Cumnock where I photographed it in April on a miners service to Barony pit, still with its "M" depot code. Although intended to move to the Isle of Bute for the summer, in May, together with GCS 222-4/6 from the same batch of Northern Counties bodied Leyland PD2/20s, it was transferred to Highland Omnibuses becoming JD6. GCS 232 retained its PD1 radiator, thus belying its true age, and operated from Inverness depot on a variety of services, including the two-hour commuter run from Tain to Inverness. It was withdrawn in December 1969 and sold to dealer Kelbie at Turriff who scrapped it. *(JS)*

Western SMT also had three Daimler CWA6s re-bodied by ECW in 1952. ASD 414 was one of 13 utility L55R Daimlers new in 1944, eight with Brush bodies and the others, including this, with austere Duple bodies. Although the remainder were rebuilt to varying degrees, and reseated to 53 upholstered seats, ASD 414 alone was re-bodied, as was a solitary Duple-bodied Daimler new the previous year, ASD 351. In common with the remainder of the Western wartime Daimlers, they continued to operate from Kilmarnock depot. ASD 414 was photographed with its original body outside the station in original condition, including wooden slatted seats. *(RG)*

The third Daimler to receive an ECW body was VS 4309, a CWA6 model with a Brush body delivered to WSMT in July 1944, but not licensed and transferred to subsidiary company Greenock Motor Services a month later. With similar VS 4310/1, it was transferred back to Western SMT's Kilmarnock depot the following year, and was photographed there in 1962. It was withdrawn in April 1963, and the other two re-bodied Daimlers in December 1962. All three were sold to dealer Millburn Motors and scrapped, having outlived their contemporaries by seven years. VS 4309 was allocated to local service K1 from Beansburn to Shortlees for a time, but unlike most of Kilmarnock's fleet, the other two never had any specific route allocation. *(JS)*

31

Unusually, four prewar Albion CX19s (XS 4771-4) with English Electric H56R bodies new to Young's Bus Services of Paisley in 1938 were also similarly re-bodied in late 1952. From a batch of six which passed to WSMT in January 1951 when Youngs were taken over, they had Gardner 6LW engines and had been used on intensive services between Glasgow and Johnstone, and Glasgow and Largs. The bodies of the two (XS 4769/70) which retained their original bodies were scrapped at Kilmarnock in 1955 and the chassis dismantled for spares. XS 4774 is seen here when new in Young's livery of orange, yellow and maroon. *(RG)*

With their new bodies, they were reallocated to a traditional Western SMT depot at Ayr, where they joined a fleet of 18 Albions with Alexander L53R bodies dating from 1949. Two of these, however, had been fitted to 1947 chassis which had originally entered service with ex-Ribble metal-framed Leyland bodies due to delayed availability of Northern Counties bodies. XS 4771-4 remained in service at Ayr and its sub-depot at Girvan until withdrawn in 1961. Three subsequently ran for Dunoon Motor Services who operated mainly seasonal services in Cowal, and XS 4773 was sold to a contractor. XS 4774 is seen again here, leaving Ayr bus station on the short journey to the village of Annbank. *(RG)*

It was more common to see utility Guys re-bodied by Eastern Coachworks, and Alexander sent six of its wartime allocation of 101 such vehicles down to Lowestoft in 1951. WG 9818/9, new in 1942 with Duple bodies, were from a batch of nine Arab Is which all retained their Gardner 5LW engines. WG 9818, photographed at Dundas Street bus station in Glasgow in 1963, had been transferred to subsidiary David Lawson in 1949, but returned in 1961. Repainted into blue with its 'Midland' fleetname, it finally left Kirkintilloch in March 1964 for Alloa depot, and was withdrawn for scrap in August. *(JS)*

David Lawson of Kirkintilloch received 13 Arab IIs with Roe bodies, and three of these (WG 9980/1 and AMS 45) were re-bodied together with AMS 46 transferred from the main Alexander fleet in 1945. All passed to Midland in May 1961when the Lawson fleet was absorbed into the main Alexander (Midland) fleet, as the W Alexander empire was split into three separate companies. AMS 46, also seen at Dundas Street bus station but in December 1962, has still to be repainted into fleet colours, and features a cowl in front of the cab to make up the extra bonnet length of the Arab II. All four were withdrawn in 1965 with AMS 46 passing to a contractor in Dundee. *(JS)*

33

WSMT subsidiary Greenock Motor Services were allocated 35 utility Guys, all with Gardner 5LW engines. Nine had Roe bodies, eight Northern Counties and eighteen Weymann. Of these, four were re-bodied with ECW bodies in 1951, including all three mark I models with Roe bodies (VS 4216/7/42). The fourth, VS 4349 with a Weymann body, seen here in GMS colours, was also sent to Lowestoft following a major accident. Two others were given new Alexander bodies and, surprisingly, two were fitted with further utility bodies from ex-London Transport Guys subsequently themselves re-bodied by Alexander. *(RG)*

VS 4349 only outlived its contemporaries by four years, being withdrawn in April 1961. It had remained at Greenock for its entire operating life as did the remainder of these vehicles, apart from those receiving second-hand bodies, VS 4355 with a Weymann body moving to Ayr and 4357 with a Park Royal body to Johnstone depot. VS 4349 was photographed in Glasgow in 1964 with Grant Brothers, a small company with school contracts which it operated in conjunction with Northern Roadways in whose livery it is painted. *(JS)*

Massey-bodied Guy Arab IIs XS 5624-7 entered service with Graham of Paisley in 1945, and 5625/6 were re-bodied by Northern Counties, the former in 1952 as seen in this picture taken at their depot in 1965. XS 5626, however, received a 'tin front' when re-bodied two years later. ABV 988 was also new with a Massey utility body, in 1944 to Blackburn Corporation, and re-bodied by East Lancs in 1954. It was acquired by Graham in August 1964 and ran for three years, making an interesting comparison with ACB 901 also new to Blackburn Corporation, in 1947 with a Northern Coachbuilders body. XS 9834 shows the 1957 version of the evolving Northern Counties body. *(JS)*

Massey utility bodies seem to have given trouble, and FTD 450 was a further Guy Arab which required re-bodying, again with an East Lancs body. Another Lancashire operator, Rawtenstall Corporation owned the vehicle, and it was sold to James Clark of Glencaple near Dumfries, entering service in December 1964. The company was taken over by WSMT the following August, but it was not operated and sold to Millburn Motors. Parked beside it at Dumfries bus station is FJA 612, a Leyland Royal Tiger new to North Western Road Car and acquired in 1962, which was to pass to McLennan of Spittalfield who converted it to front entrance. *(JS)*

35

However, new Massey bodies were also fitted to utility Guy Arabs which entered service with bodies from other coachbuilders, and subsequently required replacing. McGill of Barrhead acquired three Guy Arab IIs (CHS 254/71/2) in 1944 and one (CHS 355) in 1945, all with Park Royal H56R bodies. All were re-bodied in 1955 with Massey H58R bodies, remaining in service until August 1969 or February 1972 (CHS 271) and subsequently scrapped. *(RG)*

All the original bodies were extensively rebuilt in the McGill bodyshop in the late nineteen forties, with re-glazed windows and an illuminated panel above the destination screen, and CHS 254 and CHS 355 were fitted with Gardner 6LW engines. This was a useful measure, as McGill operated a solitary service on the Isle of Bute, under the 'Rothesay Motor Services' title from 1955 to 1965, which involved a steep climb up the rather tortuous road to Canada Hill, and in the summer these vehicles could sometimes be seen making this journey. Their usual role, however, was operating busy local services in Paisley and Barrhead. *(RG)*

East Yorkshire MS chose CH Roe when its entire fleet of 22 utility Guys was re-bodied during 1953/4, all to the required 'Beverley Bar' configuration. They were withdrawn during 1961/2, most seeing further service. GRH 193 originally entered service with a Roe body in December 1944, and was sold in June 1961 to a dealer in Dunchurch. Acquired by TD Alexander of Sheffield, it was transferred to their Arbroath operation in August 1964 and fitted with a Gardner 6LW engine. I photographed it outside their depot in July 1968 by which time it was just being used on contract work to the Angus fruit farms. Behind is SPT 77, a Weymann-bodied Guy Arab LUF. *(JS)*

Another 'Beverley Bar' configured vehicle to arrive in Scotland was GAT 62, one of a batch of Leyland TD5s (GAT 60-70) new to EYMS in October 1939 with ECW bodies, of which all but one (GAT 65 already rebuilt) were replaced by new bodies in 1948. Sold to Passenger Vehicle Disposals in Dunchurch in November 1956, it and GAT 61 reached Lowland Motors of Shettleston in 1957, passing to Scottish Omnibuses in February 1958 when the company was taken over, and given fleet numbers HH1/2. Repainted into fleet livery, they survived until August and December 1962 respectively. *(RG)*

37

Western SMT bought 25 TD4s with Leyland H52R bodies in 1936/7 (CS 4490-514) of which 21 were re-bodied with Northern Counties L53R bodies in 1949 and withdrawn in 1960. CS 4498 had been re-bodied earlier, but three escaped. CS 4511 was sold to Millburn Motors in August 1947 after an accident, but unexpectedly reappeared with rival Dodds of Troon. CS 4501/12 had been transferred to subsidiary GMS in December 1947 passing on to Rothesay MS and on return to WSMT in 1949, ran with original bodies until withdrawn in 1953. *(RG)*

When new in September 1936, CS 4505 was in the prewar livery of black and white. In April 1949, it was delicensed and dispatched to Wigan to receive its new body, running until delicensed in April 1960, latterly at Ardrossan depot. Arriving on Bute in September rather late for the busy holiday season when Dunoon Motor Services required extra vehicles, it remained for a further two years. It was photographed still in Western red and cream livery leaving for Toward Lighthouse. Central SMT also re-bodied eleven of its nineteen 39-seat Leyland TS7Ts with similar bodies, after chassis conversion. *(RG)*

The above batch was followed by 20 all-Leyland TD5s in each of the next two years (CS 7021-40 and 8041-60) of which thirty-two remained visibly unaltered. CS 8059 is shown here before delivery. Many, however, were extensively rebuilt around 1951/2, some 'reconditioned' at Alexander's bodyworks and some by Central SMT, although most in Western's headquarters in Kilmarnock. Two also went to Wigan in 1949, (CS 7026 and 8055). After being de-roofed in 1942, CS 8051 received an austerity Alexander body in April 1943 in the middle of Alexander's own batch of TS7s. Always at Kilmarnock depot, it was probably the first bus to be repainted from wartime grey into Western's new red and cream livery in late 1944. *(RG)*

Five (CS 7024/37 and 8057-9) received a more extensive refurbishment, being sent down in 1951 to ECW's premises at Irthlingborough in Northamptonshire where all major rebuilds were being carried out. They returned with ECW pattern window pans and glazing. All operated busy Glasgow services from Newton Mearns depot, being withdrawn as early as 1956, and CS 8059 was photographed on such a service. However, unrebuilt CS 8041 on Bute was withdrawn only three months before 8051 and 8055 in June 1959. Central SMT also had six TD5s and two TD7s similarly rebuilt as well as 15 TS7s, and Scottish Omnibuses three single-deckers. CS 8059 ended up being scrapped in Bird's quarry near Stratford on Avon. *(RG)*

The 'odd one out' was CS 4498, new in July 1936, whose original body was destroyed by fire in 1941. The chassis was sent to Alexander, and it reappeared in October 1942 with a new L53R body supplied by Leyland but completed by Alexander. The first of the austerity bodies was fitted in February 1943 to former TS7 WG 3447 and CS 8051 had received such a body in May. The body fitted to CS 4498 appears to have been constructed on the same basis as those on SMT's TS7s WS 8081-6 which were re-bodied earlier in the year. Allocated to Kilmarnock depot, it ran until June 1958 and was sold to Millburn Motors for scrap in August. It was photographed at Kilmarnock beside Daimler CWA6, ASD 491, with a Brush body. Both vehicles have been fitted with an illuminated panel above the destination piece to display 'Western.' *(RG)*

By contrast, Alexander had three Leylands destroyed by fire in 1944, but they did not receive their new Alexander austerity bodies until March 1946, after the single-deck conversions had been re-bodied. WG 8681, a 1939 TD5, and WG 9183/90, which were 1940 TD7s, originally had Leyland bodies, but did not outlive their unre-bodied contemporaries. All passed into Midland ownership in 1961, WG 8681 being withdrawn at the end of the year. WG 9190, which was photographed at Milngavie depot in April 1963, was withdrawn for scrap at the end of December, along with unre-bodied 9195 which saw further use with Highland Omnibuses. *(JS)*

40

A further vehicle whose original body was destroyed by fire was Scottish Omnibuses first Daimler Fleetline 9961 SF (fleet number DD961) ordered by Baxter of Airdrie before the takeover in December 1962, but not delivered until October 1963, when it entered service at Edinburgh depot. Photographed at the bus station in June 1964, it was, unusually, not on the long service to Glasgow via Bathgate. Transferred to the former Baxter fleet in October, it was painted into their colours and given fleet number 79. Burnt out in May 1965, it was sent to Alexander for a replacement body. *(JS)*

Returning to the Baxter fleet in their livery, it was converted for OMO operation, initially on Sundays, and repainted into 'Lothian' green colours in late 1978 reverting to its original fleet number. The original Baxter Victoria Road depot in Airdrie closed in March 1979, and it, together with its identical 'replacement' DVA 680C (DD80), were transferred to the SOL depot nearby in January. However, the small borders depot at Peebles with OMO operation used a double-decker on a school contract, and both were transferred there in March. DD961 was photographed in September and withdrawn in November, but DD80 survived for a further year. *(JS)*

41

Another bus to require a similar replacement body early in its life was Highland Omnibuses Leyland Leopard VST 753L (JL3) new in June 1973 with an Alexander DP49F body. A month later it was involved in a serious accident en route to Ullapool, and did not reappear until April 1976 with its new body, in a revised coach livery. One of a batch of four coaches (JL2-5) bought for tours and express services, they were transferred to Alexander Northern the following year as NPE56-9, and immediately downgraded to service work. The other three were operated as B53F, but VST 753L continued as DP49F in coach livery and is seen here at Aberdeen bus station in 1983. *(JS)*

From 1964 to 1975, Western SMT had a policy of specifying 49-seat dual-purpose Alexander bodies for its Leopards, and RSD 732J was such a coach new in 1971 as ML2341. In May 1974 it was burnt out, and reappeared in June 1975 with a multibay 53-seat body. In May 1981, it moved to Highland Omnibuses as L4, and was photographed at Dunbeath outstation in May 1983 where it was parked overnight for a school run into Wick in the morning. Remaining in Caithness, it was withdrawn in October, and sold to Meredith of Malpas, eventually ending up with Shearing's Timeline operation in Manchester, and passing into preservation. *(JS)*

In 1959, forty-nine AEC Reliances arrived for Scottish Omnibuses, of which 29 had Park Royal 41-seat bodies, with twenty being in coach livery (SWS 690-709) with matching fleet numbers B690-709. When new, B698-708 were allocated to Edinburgh depot, and being dual-purpose vehicles were used in a variety of roles, from day tours to express services on which B698 was deployed here, and even service work as Scottish Omnibuses was perpetually short of vehicles. On 7th July 1962, it had its first major accident near Cramond Brig Hotel on the A90 Queensferry Road on the outskirts of Edinburgh, and its body was scrapped by local dealer Locke. *(RG)*

On 31st March 1963, it returned to service at Edinburgh depot with a new 49-seat Alexander Y type body in the same batch as B923-42 which were being delivered. Unbelievably, two years later it fell through a market garden onto the main Edinburgh to Glasgow railway line near Maybury, only two miles from where it was previously wrecked. This time, it only required a replacement front, and returned to service in July 1965 at Dalkeith depot where I photographed it in 1972. It was also sold to Locke (along with B708) in March 1973, both being scrapped. Interestingly, apart from B700 which also had a major accident in June 1969 and was scrapped by Locke, the remainder of the batch survived until 1975, only B696 being recorded with a further operator. *(JS)*

43

Scottish Omnibuses final batch of AEC Regal IVs in 1953 consisted of eight 30-seat toilet coaches with Alexander bodies for the Edinburgh to London service (KSC 532-9) and seventeen vehicles of similar appearance with thirty-eight seats for tours and the 'two day' London service. This less austere style was, however, only produced that year. Unfortunately, KSC 533, seen here in the original livery with a cream roof only, sustained major damage in an accident in 1956, and was returned to Alexander for a replacement body, reappearing in March 1957. *(RG)*

The style of body was similar to an AEC Reliance exhibited at the 1955 Motor Show, NSF 543 with a lightweight bus outline body shell, and these vehicles were the only ones to receive this design. Returning to the London service, it was soon transferred to Airdrie depot for use on a Glasgow to Birmingham service. This was operated in conjunction with Northern Roadways under their licence against a complex competitive background. Later KSC 533 was used on a variety of express services and was photographed at Coatbridge Cross in 1964. Withdrawn with the rest of the batch in December 1966, it passed to a local contractor Watson ending up for scrap with Tiger at Salsburgh. *(JS)*

Another coach used on Anglo-Scottish services was Western SMT NCS 117W, a Volvo B10M-61 with a Duple Dominant III C44FT body, one of a batch of twelve new in 1981. Passing to Clydeside Scottish in 1986, it was converted to Dominant IV configuration. In August 1991, it was acquired by Allander Coaches of Milngavie, and re-bodied with an East Lancs B51F body in August 1992. The company was developing a competitive network of local services in Clydebank and Dumbarton, branded as 'Loch Lomond Coaches', and it was photographed in November 1992 on service to Balloch on the shores of Loch Lomond. In 1997, it was sold to Rossendale Transport who re-registered it PJI 9173. *(JS)*

Further members of this batch to be re-bodied were NCS 116W which received a new Duple Caribbean body in 1983, and NCS 121W and GGE 127X from the 1982 delivery which were also re-bodied by East Lancs, in 1994 as DP51F, and were the first vehicles to appear in Stagecoach livery after buying WSMT from its management. With their fourth registrations as VLT 154 and ESU 435 respectively, they were photographed in 1998 at Ardrossan depot in Clyde Coaster livery for the service from Greenock down the Clyde Coast to Ayr. Parked beside is their unique Volvo B10B with a Wright Endurance body M151 FGB, new as AI Motor Services M1 ABO. *(JS)*

45

A further 'London Coach' to receive a second body was Western SMT AEC Regal IV HWS 929, one of fourteen (HWS 927-40) numbered 920-33, new in 1951 with Alexander C30F bodies. In 1955 it was one of eight converted for service work at Inchinnan depot with removal of the toilet and reseating with 40 dual-purpose seats, for both local and express work. Over the years, the external appearance of them all changed to differing degrees with removal of chrome work and modifications to grilles, but on March 24th1959 HWS 929 was burnt out. However, I photographed two of that batch in January 1964 stored for disposal at Townholm depot in Kilmarnock, parked beside CSD 889 one of two 1950 Guy Arab IIIs with Northern Counties bodies. *(JS)*

All fourteen coaches saw further use, seven passing to Highland Omnibuses. HWS 929 had been sold to Alex Bell Ltd possibly as an insurance write off, rather than as usual to Millburn Motors like the rest of the batch. It reappeared the following year with a small Glasgow operator A&G Taylor who acquired two ECW C39F bodies from a batch of Tilling Regal IVs (LYM 728-32) new in 1952 and re-bodied in 1960 to MW style, one of which was LYM 732 which was used for HWS 929, and it was not disposed of until 1977 when it went to a dealer in nearby Bailleston. LYM 732 is now preserved, HWS 929 also I believe went south for preservation, and I may have glimpsed it in Leicester bus station on a service around 1982. *(RG)*

46

Further use of bodies from vehicles re-bodied for fleet modernisation was common in the Scottish Bus Group both before and after the war. Scottish Omnibuses sent 45 AEC Regals, new in 1948/9 to Blackpool to receive Burlingham Seagull bodies in 1953 and 1954. Sixteen of their Alexander bodies were fitted to other chassis in the Scottish Bus Group, including three prewar AECs with Duple bodies acquired by Alexander with the fleet of Sutherland of Peterhead in 1950. AV 7359 had a C32R body, heavily rebuilt by Sutherland by the time it was photographed in 1952 as were the others acquired by Alexander. *(AC)*

It went down to the Alexander headquarters at Larbert in January 1954 returning with its new body in May, with the original scrapped by a dealer in Falkirk. However, in October 1955, it was sold to Tait and Park of Stromness in Orkney who ran it for ten more years, and it was photographed leaving Kirkwall by Robert Grieves. Unre-bodied AV 7358, new in 1935, was also withdrawn at the same time. However, AV 8332 at Rosehearty, new in 1936, and AAV 844 at Peterhead, new in 1938, survived with their new bodies until 1961 and September 1964 respectively, with the latter transferring to Alexander Northern, and repainted into fleet colours. *(RG)*

47

Highland Omnibuses also fitted ex-Scottish Omnibuses Alexander bodies to four Guy Arabs new with Strachan B34F bodies; BST 669 in 1947, CST 697 in 1948 and DST 283/4 in 1949. While the former two were service buses, the latter arrived in the cream and red coach livery with high-back seats. DST 283 was photographed with its new body. It was the last to be re-bodied, arriving in August 1958 with 30 coach seats from the 1949 batch. Based in Caithness, it was withdrawn in 1963 with DST 284, and both passed to showmen. BST 669 and CST 697 both reappeared in 1955, the latter at Dingwall, and were withdrawn in 1962 and 1963, at the same time as their unre-bodied contemporaries. *(RG)*

DST 284 returned in June 1955 with its new B35F body which was known to come from GSF 703, and was photographed at Dounreay nuclear facility in Caithness in September 1961 parked beside EST 395. It had brought staff from the town of Wick an hour's distance away, whereas EST 395, which was the pride of the fleet, had come on contract from John O' Groats where it was outstationed. It too was new with a Strachan body in 1951 but with 38 seats and a Gardner 6LW engine, and had been extensively rebuilt. It remained in daily service until April 1969, when it was withdrawn and sold to a contractor in Fraserburgh. *(JS)*

The Scottish Omnibuses order of 40 AEC Regal IIIs in 1949 was composed of 20 with half-cab Burlingham bodies with 35 dual-purpose seats (GSF 684-703) and 20 with Alexander bodies (GSF 704-23). With one exception, those with Burlingham bodies completed fifteen to sixteen years in service, initially on long distance services and tours, but latterly many ended up in the border depots. GSF 689 was such a bus, moving to Galashiels in 1958, and was photographed in the village of Melrose in 1963 while operating from the sub-depot there at which four buses were garaged overnight. It was delicensed in May 1965 and sold to a contractor, who ran it for a further three years. *(JS)*

The exception was GSF 693 which after a crash, ironically received an Alexander C35F body in 1955 from a bus in the same batch that was being re-bodied with a Burlingham Seagull body. It ran with this body for ten years, and was also delicensed in May 1965, passing initially to Edinburgh dealer Locke, but was scrapped. Allocated to Galashiels depot since re-bodying, it was photographed at the congested bus station on a Saturday afternoon in 1963 after arriving in on the B65 service from Melrose. It was operating out of the ten-vehicle sub-depot at Selkirk, where it was normally garaged overnight. *(JS)*

49

Fifteen of the 1949 AEC Regal IIIs with composite Alexander bodies (GSF 704-18) were initially operated on the Edinburgh to London and express services, and were fitted with 30 coach seats. However, with the arrival of the 26 AEC Regal IVs with toilets in 1951, they were no longer required for such work, and with a demand for modern looking coaches, they were re-bodied with Burlingham Seagull bodies in 1954. Initially. shared between Edinburgh and Airdrie depots, they were later cascaded down, some to the borders, and GSF 717 was photographed in Kelso square on a private hire in June 1965. It was delicensed in March 1966 passing to the contractor Cruden of Musselburgh. *(JS)*

The final five (GSF 719-23) were fitted with 35 low-back seats from new, and used on stage carriage work throughout their fifteen-year life. As such they were never re-bodied, and operated from Airdrie depot for much of their lives, with GSF 720/2/3 being transferred to Broxburn depot in March 1963. GSF 720 was photographed at Edinburgh bus station the following year waiting to return to the West Lothian village of Oakbank, once home of an oil company that no longer exists. It was delicensed in August 1964 and scrapped. It is interesting to note that all forty vehicles were withdrawn between 1964 and 1966, and those re-bodied with Burlingham Seagull bodies did not outlast some of those new with half-cab bodies. *(JS)*

The preceding batch of single-deck bodies from the Alexander coachworks also went to SMT as the company was then called, but were fitted to twenty-seven Leyland TS6s from 1933 (FS 5599-619/21-6), the missing one being burnt out, as was FS 5581. The remaining twenty-five arrived with Burlingham bodies similar to the AEC Regals delivered that year and survived until 1961 whereas the Alexander batch was withdrawn in 1959/60. FS 5609 was fitted with its C35F body in 1949 and was photographed at Stirling Bus Station still in coach livery and without a depot plate. Latterly at Bathgate depot, it was withdrawn in March 1959, passing to Locke and scrapped. *(RG)*

In the preceding year, SMT purchased 60 AEC Regals (FS 2251-310) with fleet numbers B14-73, all with Alexander B34R bodies. With the exception of FS 2274, destroyed in an accident in 1934, they were all re-bodied and all remained in service with SMT for at least twenty-five years. 22 received new all-metal Alexander dual-purpose bodies starting with FS 2297 in 1946 and FS 2277 being the last in August 1947. By contrast, Burlingham fitted service bus bodies to a further 30 throughout 1948. Photographed in a line-up shortly after delivery, the destination screens display some of the more distant locations to which they would run. *(RG)*

However, in 1948, six were sent to Glasgow bodybuilder Croft who had been involved with renovation work on a variety of buses during the war with on occasions constructing new bodies. The firm also built a number of new bodies on single-deckers and double-deckers until 1951. FS 2267/91/5/9/300/10 were all withdrawn ten years later, with five passing to contractors, and three surviving to the end of 1960 when over twenty-eight years old. However, FS 2310, seen here in Selkirk with its rather austere body on a 'Mill Service', did not see further service. *(S)*

The one exception was FS 2263. New in April 1932, its Alexander B34R body was replaced with a Burlingham C32R body only a year newer in 1946. This was from a batch of six AEC Regals used on the London service which were delicensed in 1940, reappearing in 1944 with Alexander L53R bodies. However, it was classified as rebuilt to B35F by SMT in 1952 around the time when new bodies were being constructed at Marine Gardens, and the accompanying picture would suggest that little of the original body remains. Operating from Edinburgh depot (code A), it was sold in March 1959, passing to a showman and was still in use five years later. *(RG)*

Alexander were also in urgent need of single-deckers when the war ended, and chose 25 Leyland LT5A chassis from various sources, and designed a 35-seat single-decker variant of the austerity double-deck design, fitting them at the end of 1945. Some already had Leyland 8.6 engines, others were fitted with AEC 7.7 and one with a Leyland 7.4. All were withdrawn by 1960. Only one, WG 3260, operated in Fife, and I photographed it at St Andrews bus station on front line service in August 1956. Now preserved, it was new in March 1935 with an Alexander B36F body, re-bodied and fitted with an 8.6 engine in October 1945 and withdrawn in June 1958. *(JS)*

Western SMT urgently required coaches to reinstate its Glasgow to London service, and also acquired Leyland Lions, in total thirty from various operators. By contrast, they were fitted with Brush C30F bodies in 1946 and Leyland 7.4 engines. Apart from seven sold in 1948, they were downgraded to tours and later service work, most being converted to B35F, and all withdrawn by 1959. VS 2725, seen here in black and white colours when re-bodied in March 1946, was an LT7, new to subsidiary GMS in 1935 with a Leyland B39R body. It operated for subsidiary Dunlop between 1948 and 1949, and latterly in bus livery as B35F with a folding door and an AEC engine. *(RG)*

The Caledonian OC taken over by WSMT in 1950 also re-bodied Leyland Lions, but with ECW bodies in late 1948. Six were LT2s new in 1931 with Leyland B26F bodies and two LT5s new in 1932 with ECOC bodies. Rebuilt during the war and converted to a Gardner 4LW engine, with their new bodies they remained in service with WSMT until 1957. SM 8853, an LT2 seen here with a Covrad radiator, is thought to have run on producer gas during the war, but was fitted with a 4LW engine in May 1947. It was re-bodied in February 1949, withdrawn in July1957, and via dealers ended up with contractor Cruden in 1959, already 28 years old. *(RG)*

Caledonian only re-bodied two of its 33 Dennis Lancets with ECW bodies, although many were rebuilt during the war. DSM 453 seen here at the fishing village of Port William opposite the Mull of Galloway, and a couple of miles from the holiday village of Monreith, was new in May 1938 with a Brush B32F body. Despite having its body reconditioned by Croft in 1943, it required a new body in March 1949. WSMT allocated it to the Stranraer area where it ran until withdrawn in March 1957, passing to Davies of Leeswood. AEC Regent BAG152 parked beside it had been transferred down from Cumnock to the former Caledonian territory after the take-over. *(AC)*

AA partner Dodds of Troon acquired a Bristol L5G with a replacement ECW body from Bristol Omnibus Company, specifically for an OMO service that operated under a low bridge to the nearby village of Barassie. LHT 903 was an L6B chassis new in 1948 with an ECW DP31R body. In 1957 it received a body from a prewar Bristol J chassis which had been rebodied in 1951. This was to B35F specification, converted for OMO operation, and Dodds obtained it in December 1962 through the dealer North of Leeds. It remained on this busy service until June 1968 when sold to a local builder in Irvine, and was photographed intact in a yard nine years later. *(JS)*

Another post war single-decker to receive a second body was Leyland PS1 FDK 908 of Mitchell of Luthermuir, seen here at their garage in September 1965, two years before Alexander (Northern) took over the company. New to Yelloway Motor Services of Rochdale in August 1947 with a Trans United C33F body, it was acquired by Mitchell in 1956. In 1961, it received the 8ft wide 1950 Duple C31F body from ex-Ribble TS7 RN 7768 obtained from Millburn Motors in Preston, but not operated. Withdrawn in January 1967, it was sold to a Boys Brigade company in Glasgow. The rear of Burlingham bodied PS1 JC 9033 is seen in the garage. *(JS)*

55

Western SMT acquired the long established operator Paton of Renfrew in August 1979, and operated all ten Leopards, which were painted into fleet livery and numbered 1-10. The first six had Willowbrook bodies, but 7-10 (SSU 396/7R and YHS 281/2S) had Duple B55F bodies, and SSU 397R is seen here when new at the Renfrew Ferry terminus. 6-10 were transferred to Western's operation in Islay when they took over all the services in May 1980. This operation was later transferred to Midland Scottish in June 1985, and to local operator Mundell in October 1986. The four Duple-bodied vehicles moved to the mainland, with YHS 281/2S allocated to Oban depot. *(JS)*

Their subsequent fate then varied. SSU 397R new in 1976, roamed on loan to Linlithgow, then SMT at Livingston finally settling at Falkirk in February 1987. However, in June, it received a 1974 Alexander body from a withdrawn Fife Leopard XXA 862M, and was photographed the following month on a local service in Falkirk. It was withdrawn in 1991, passing to Lanarkshire operator Whitelaw of Stonehouse. YHS 281S was destroyed in a fire at Oban depott in November 1990, and YHS 282S passed to Kelvin Central Buses where its body underwent extensive renovation to strengthen the rear panels and survived to 1997. SSU 396R was withdrawn as early as May 1988. *(JS)*

56

It was common for smaller operators to transfer newer or sometimes older bodies to chassis where the original bodies had deteriorated prematurely, particularly those constructed during the war. Paton of Renfrew pursued this policy sometimes through the medium of the dealer Millburn Motors. In December 1949, Paton acquired the non standard 'unfrozen' Leyland TS11s DGE 950/1 with utility Burlingham B36F bodies from David MacBrayne. Entering service in wartime grey colours, DGE 951 is seen in a short-lived cream and black livery featured in 1947, with a silhouette of the Highland warrior under the black 'MacBraynes' fleetname. *(RG)*

As the mainstay of the 147-mile-long trunk route between Glasgow and Campbeltown, which incorporated the notorious 'Rest And Be Thankful', they had laboured during the war years, often overladen with standing passengers. Now rendered surplus by the arrival of new Maudslays, MacBraynes had no further use for utility vehicles. However, DGE 950, unaltered, ran for a further eight years with Paton before being sold for scrap. DGE 951, however, received a second-hand Alexander B39F body in 1956, probably from SMT's 1940 batch of Leyland TS8s (DSC 302-21). It was last licensed to Paton in July 1960. *(RG)*

57

Larger operators also replaced unsatisfactory bodies, particularly those constructed during the war from unseasoned timber, and Western SMT fitted contemporary bodies to a few of its utility vehicles. Guy Arab II ASD 710 new in June 1945 with a Weymann L55R body, however, received two replacement bodies within a period of four years, the third being older than the first two. Seen here at Ayr bus station in 1950, it shows no external features of refurbishment, but the radiator has been embellished to the high standards of the regular driver. Fitted with a Gardner 6LW engine, it was used on busy country services, such as to the village of Drongan close to the Ayrshire coalfields. *(AC)*

Western SMT fitted three of the Weymann H56R bodies from former London Transport Guy Arabs to its own vehicles, with the acquired chassis going to Alexander for new lowbridge bodies. These were ASD 710, ASD 22, a 1942 Guy Arab I with itself a Weymann H56R body, and VS 4355, a 1945 Guy Arab II from the fleet of Greenock Motor Services, also with a Weymann L55R body. These came from a batch of seven with HGC registrations, most of which ran in service for at least a summer with their original bodies after some remedial work and ASD 710 has had an illuminated panel fitted above the destination screen. Only the identity of the body transferred to ASD 22 in November 1952 is known, HGC 208. *(RM)*

58

After four years, the second Weymann body on ASD 710 was replaced by a Northern Counties L53R body in June 1957 from ASD 407, a 1944 Guy Arab II delicensed a year earlier to allow its chassis to be used to construct a tow wagon. Ironically, ASD 404/5, with the same body, had already been re-bodied in 1951. Seen here with its third body on an Ayr local service, ASD 710 has now lost its original radiator, but the body has undergone reconstruction in the past. Finishing its sixteen year life at Ayr depot in November 1961, it was then put into store and finally sold for scrap the following July, but still with a six month COF. *(RG)*

ASD 407, the donor vehicle, also spent its early life at Ayr depot like all the utility Guys, but ended up at Greenock depot where it was photographed beside two other Guys which had received new Alexander bodies in 1952. HGC 152 was former LTE G112 which theoretically could be the one which donated its Weymann body to ASD 710, but we will never know. Beside it is VS 4333 a Guy Arab II new with a Weymann L55R body to GMS, and re-bodied along with VS 4346. Interestingly, as well as VS 4355, mentioned previously, VS 4357 also received an ex-LTE body in 1953, but a Park Royal body from one of four with GLL registrations whose bodies cannot be accounted for. *(RG)*

Two further Guy Arabs from the 1945 batch new to the original Western SMT fleet also received new 7ft 6in wide Alexander bodies in 1953, ASD 701 and 705. The bodies were similar to the 8ft wide version on the recently delivered Daimlers. They too were new with Weymann L55R bodies and Gardner 6LW engines, and used on longer distance services. ASD 705 seen here at Ayr bus station was the regular performer on the flagship service from Ayr to Glasgow, and also shows little external evidence of refurbishment. Beside it is ASD 707 from the same batch, but with a metal-framed Northern Counties H56R body to the more 'relaxed' style, and it remained in service unmodified until June 1961. *(AC)*

Surprisingly, ASD 701 and 705, although given new bodies, didn't survive any longer. ASD 705, seen again at Ayr bus station and due to depart for another Ayrshire village, was delicensed in April 1960. Transferred to Highland Omnibuses in October, it was, however, returned three months later, moved to Greenock and finally withdrawn in November 1961. It did, however, see further use with a contractor in Aberdeen, not finally leaving service until 1966. Also in the photograph is the unique Guy Arab ASD 253 with its Leyland style reconstruction of its Massey body. There were four other vehicles in the 1945 batch whose Weymann bodies were simply rebuilt which were withdrawn in 1957, and one, ASD 708, ran with a London contractor until December 1959. *(RG)*

HGC 152, seen with its new Alexander body in a previous picture, ran with its original Weymann body for a year after it had received attention in the body shop, even having an illuminated panel fitted above the destination screen. Without an allocated fleet number, it was photographed at Greenock, despite the destination. It returned there in January 1953 still with a Gardner 5LW engine and with seven others continued to run on the hilly terrain of the local services there for the next ten years. Sold to Millburn Motors in July 1963, it passed to a fruit farmer in Angus for staff transport. *(RG)*

A further two of the 19 ex-London Guys re-bodied by Alexander were allocated to Johnstone depot, but the remaining nine ended up in the Dumfries area, subsequently fitted with Gardner 6LW engines. They were confined to the Solway depots, with five allocated to Carlisle, three to Lockerbie, and one to Annan, seen here parked behind the depot off its school run in April 1963. GYL 335 was one of eight former London Transport Guys with Park Royal bodies delivered to WSMT, all of which received new Alexander bodies, but the fate of its original body is unknown. Withdrawn in April 1964, it was sold to a dealer in Rothwell. *(JS)*

Three of these Alexander re-bodied Guys allocated to the former Caledonian territory were transferred to Highland Omnibuses in 1963, after having platform doors fitted in the body shop at Dumfries depot. The result was a unique combination of a 7ft 6in' wide Alexander body of this style with a platform door. Moving from the south west to the far north of Scotland, these were a necessity, and the trio (HGC 146-8) operated in Caithness for a further four years. HGC 147 was photographed leaving Thurso garage to take up an early morning run to the nuclear reactor at Dounreay. HGC 148 had the distinction of being the furthest north double-decker in Scotland, outstationed at Mey to bring children from John O' Groats into school at Thurso. *(JS)*

A more enterprising form of re-bodying occurred to the second batch of former London Guys to be acquired by WSMT in 1953. Eight received 1947 vintage Croft L53R bodies transferred from seven Leyland TD1s and a TD2 inherited with the Caledonian fleet. Withdrawn in 1961, all but one saw further use. GYL 317, new to LTE in May 1945 as G178, received the body from TM 3846, a 1928 TD1 in November 1953. Photographed at Carlisle, it was withdrawn in June 1961 passing to Service Coaches of Bebside. Parked beside it is XS 5547, one of three Guys new to Youngs of Paisley in 1943 with Pickering bodies, of which it was the only one to be re-bodied by ECW in 1951. *(RG)*

It was not only Western SMT Guys that received second-hand bodies from former London Transport Guys which were re-bodied. A solitary Daimler CWA6 (ASD 967), the last utility Daimler to come, arrived in January 1946 with a Brush highbridge body. Apart from the first four Daimler CWG5s which had Massey bodies, all the others, including eleven with Brush bodies, had been to lowbridge design. It had received some refurbishment including fitting with the ubiquitous illuminated panel and operated daily on Kilmarnock town services. However, to my surprise, when looking out of the infirmary window after having my appendix out, it passed by the hospital with a completely different body. *(RG)*

In December 1952, the Park Royal body off GXE 552, new to London Transport in February 1945, was fitted to ASD 967. Not only was it older, but of less relaxed design, and with half drop windows was clearly a utility vehicle. However, the body had been reconditioned when GXE 552 arrived from the south, and it had operated from Newton Mearns depot during much of 1952. There were still three Park Royal bodies (from GLL 578/81/90) stored in WSMT's auxilliary garage in Kilmarnock in August 1954, but they were never used and scrapped in 1956. ASD 967 was finally delicensed in November 1957 and sold to Millburn Motors, where I saw it being scrapped in April 1958. *(AC)*

In 1949, four utility Daimlers with Massey bodies (DWS 83, a CWG5, and DWS 420-2 which were CWA6s) in the Edinburgh Corporation fleet also received second-hand replacement bodies from Guys, only to have these replaced by new Alexander bodies in 1954. The remaining vehicle of that batch DWS 82, however, retained its original Massey body, which was extensively rebuilt that year by Campbell Brothers of Whitburn, a small West Lothian coachbuilder who operated a fleet of coaches. In addition, between 1948 and 1954, they rebuilt a variety of bodies for local bus operators as well as constructing half a dozen new single-deck bodies. *(RD)*

The bodies transferred from the Guys also required renovation, and in the case of DWS 421, this was also a Massey body which was rebuilt in the Corporation's own workshops before placing on the Daimler chassis. The other three all received bodies constructed by Pickering of Wishaw, and these also went to Campbell for renovation before fitting to the Daimlers. DWS 83 received its body from Guy Arab I DWS 126 in April 1949, and it in turn received a new Northern Counties body continuing in service until 1962. DWS 83 then received its second replacement body, by Alexander, in 1954, and was not withdrawn until 1967. *(RD)*

Alexander bodies were fitted to a total of sixteen Edinburgh utility Daimlers in 1954, and those with AEC engines had them replaced by 5LW Gardner units. Being relatively underpowered, they tended to be used as 'rush hour extras' and I used to time my journey to school in the morning to catch one of these rather ungainly machines. They were fitted with Edinburgh 'quasi Leyland' glass-fibre fronts in 1959 and the entire batch sold to a dealer in Barnsley in December 1967. Interestingly, one Daimler escaped having an Alexander body, as after an accident in 1945, it was fitted with a rebuilt single-deck English Electric body from a 1933 Morris Dictator. *(RG)*

The iconic Edinburgh utility vehicle was probably the lightweight Duple-bodied former London Transport Guy Arab, of which sixty arrived in 1953. The original bodies were scrapped, and the chassis reconditioned by Guy Motors to accommodate an 8ft wide body, all being fitted with Gardner 5LW engines. The first two had Duple bodies built at Hendon, but the remainder were assembled at the Kegworth premises formerly owned by Nudd and Lockyer, with the lower shell being produced by Duple. JWS 618, photographed in Princes Street, was new in July 1953 as GYL 347 (G208) and withdrawn for scrap in 1967. Apart from preserved JWS 594, they all went to dealers in 1967 or 1969. *(RG)*

65

Croft Engineering of Glasgow also reconditioned bus bodies during the war, and built new bodies until 1951. Cowieson of Glasgow, however, was a long established firm building double-deckers from 1929 until 1938. In 1935, Glasgow Corporation bought 20 Albion SP81 (YS 2001-20) with Gardner 6LW engines and Cowieson H52R bodies, as seen in this line-up when new. The 1936 arrivals, however, (YS 2081-110) had Beardmore engines soon replaced by Leyland units. In 1944, Caledonian purchased YS 2003/7/95/110 and these were re-bodied by Croft with metal-framed bodies in 1947 at the same time as seven Leyland TD1s and TD2. *(RG)*

In 1950, these Albions passed to WSMT and YS 2095 is shown here on a Dumfries local service with its Croft body, an illuminated 'Western' panel and a 'Covrad' replacement radiator for its Leyland engine, thus looking identical to a TD1. YS 2003 and 2007 retained their Gardner engines and Albion radiators. All four Albions continued in daily use at Dumfries, with YS 2095 the last to be withdrawn in July 1957. Too late for these bodies to be replaced on other chassis, the vehicles were broken up by dealers for scrap, YS 2095 going to Millburn Motors and merely a shell when I saw it in there in December. *(RG)*

Croft Engineering was actually selected by the Ministry of War Transport to recondition and build new bus bodies, and there has always been doubt about those on the three Western SMT Leyland TD2s (AG 8239/57/9) which outlived the rest of that batch by five years. New with Leyland H48R bodies in 1932, they were 'rebuilt' during the war with AG 8257/9 returning with lowbridge bodies. The bodies, however, were not to Croft's utility style and some of the work may have been carried out by WSMT. AG 8259 is recorded as being relicensed in May 1944 with its new body. AG 8239 I personally recall as highbridge, but otherwise identical to AG 8257 seen here in Greenock in 1951. *(RG)*

Croft's utility bodies were to austerity specification, and 15 were constructed between 1943 and 1946 for early Leylands, six on Caledonian TD1s and one for subsidiary Dunlop which all passed to WSMT joining its solitary TD1. In 1939, Sheffield Corporation sold to Paisley and District Leyland TD1 WE 8776 which received a new Croft L51R body in 1944. Withdrawn in 1946, it later reached Greig of Inverness whom Alexander acquired in 1947. Passing with Alexander's Inverness operation to Highland Omnibuses in January 1952, it was never repainted, and was photographed later that year at the bus station shortly before withdrawal. *(AC)*

In addition to the seven Daimlers and two Albions fitted with second-hand bodies from Ribble re-bodied Leyland TD4s in order to get them into service quickly, two utility Guys also received Leyland bodies in 1948 as their original bodies had deteriorated beyond repair. These were Weymann (ASD 23) and Massey (ASD 94) both subsequently re-bodied by ECW in 1951. ASD 23 is recorded as returning to service in July after being out of service for six months. The interim bodies were Leyland metal-framed, similar to that seen on VS 4364 on page 5, and ASD 94 is seen near its home depot of Ayr in inclement weather. *(RG)*

ASD 94 received its final. (third), body in September 1951 continuing at Ayr depot on local services until withdrawn ten years later, finally running with Pearsons Motorways of Walsall until February 1965. It was photographed, however, at Dumfries beside the WSMT office on the Whitesands. ASD 95, however, had its Massey body rebuilt in Western's own bodyshop in December 1949, using Leyland/Alexander framing, as seen in a later picture, being withdrawn in June 1957. ASD 23 was joined by ASD 20 (see later) and 21 both also re-bodied with ECW H56R bodies for Ayr town services. *(RG)*

68

Another bus to receive a second-hand prewar Leyland body was HD 7826, a Leyland PD2 new in 1948 to Yorkshire Woollen District with a Brush H56R body, which was acquired by Laurie of Hamilton in 1959, together with HD 7827. Following an accident shortly after acquisition, it was re-bodied with the 1939 Leyland H52R body from FOF 307, one of two Leyland TD6s purchased from Birmingham Corporation in 1952. The other, FOF 288, donated its body to DUS 437 an ex-Glasgow Corporation Daimler CWA6. In October 1961, Central SMT acquired Laurie's operation, with HD 7826 and 7827 continuing in service until 1965 and 1962 respectively. *(JS)*

Another postwar bus to receive a second hand prewar body was BVD 570, a Guy Arab II new to Laurie (Chieftain) of Hamilton in 1945 with yet another utility Massey body which had deteriorated prematurely and required replacement. This body came from HF 6246, one of five Leyland TD4s with Metro Cammell bodies purchased by Wallasey Corporation in 1937, and sold to Laurie in 1952. The other four HF 6208/10/22/30 were placed in service, and the body of HF 6246 transferred immediately. *(RG)*

It was more common for smaller operators to obtain a contemporary body for replacement after an accident, should the damaged vehicle not receive a new body, and Paton of Renfrew was proficient at sourcing replacement bodies when required. JNU 556 was a Guy Arab II new in 1945 with a Weymann L55R body which had come north in 1957 from Chesterfield Corporation Transport. The following year it had a major accident and was photographed at the depot before the body was removed. *(rg)*

The replacement came from another Guy Arab II new in the same year, but with a Northern Counties H56R body, GYL 396, new to London Transport as G257. It had been acquired by Western SMT in 1953, but because its metal-framed body was in such good condition, it did not require replacement, and it was allocated to Ayr depot for the town services. Delicensed in July 1957, it was briefly on loan to Central SMT, before returning to storage until April 1958, when it was sold to dealer Millburn Motors before passing to Paton in June. As re-bodied, JNU 556 operated for another three years until withdrawn in September 1961. *(RG)*

Another Guy to receive a replacement body from Western SMT was GYE 87, an Arab II with a Gardner 5LW engine and a Park Royal body new to London Transport in 1945 as G143. It was sold to North (dealer) Leeds in 1953, and acquired by Dodds of Troon in August, where it underwent a partial body overhaul, as seen in this picture. Withdrawn two years later, it did not return to service until November 1961 with an Eastern Coachworks body from ASD 20, a Guy Arab I also with a Gardner 5LW engine. *(RG)*

ASD 20 was one of six Guys new in 1942, and ASD 22 and 23, both re-bodied, have been referred to earlier. All had Weymann bodies, but ASD 18 and 19 kept their original bodies, albeit rebuilt. ASD 20, 21 and 23 for their third body, all received ECW H56R bodies in 1951 and ASD 20 was withdrawn ten years later, reaching Dodds in September 1961. With its ECW body, GYE 87 resumed operating for Dodds, being photographed at Irvine in December 1963, after operating a local service. It was withdrawn in November 1966 and sold to a dealer in Bellshill in Lanarkshire. *(JS)*

Another Guy in the Dodds fleet to receive a replacement Eastern Coach Works body from a Western SMT Guy was DUS 424, an Arab II with a Gardner 6LW engine and a Northern Counties body new to Glasgow Corporation in 1944. It was sold to Gray (dealer) Braidwood in 1951 and acquired by Dodds in April 1952, when it underwent refurbishment, and was photographed at the depot beside CAG 801. Later delicensed, it reappeared in June 1962 with an Eastern Coach Works body from XS 5564, an Arab II also with a Gardner 6LW engine. It was new to Youngs of Paisley in 1944 with a Massey body, also re-bodied in 1951 and withdrawn in 1961 passing to Dodds with ASD 20. *(RG)*

With its new body DUS 424 operated until July 1967 when it was sold to a builder in Irvine. It was photographed at the depot in Troon in December 1963 beside GYE 87, and two other re-bodied Guys. GRH 146 was an Arab II new to EYMS in 1944 with a Brush body and re-bodied by Roe in 1953, passing to Dodds in 1961 along with GRH 145. JEH 482 was also an Arab II, new to Potteries MT in 1943 with a Strachan L55R body and re-bodied by Northern Counties in 1952, passing to Dodds in 1960. At the far end is OKM 317 new in 1951 as an AEC demonstrator with a lightweight Saunders-Roe body which is now preserved. *(JS)*

A more complex series of re-bodyings occurred in the Dodds fleet, involving Guy Arabs with Park Royal bodies. The vehicles concerned were CAG 800/1 and CSD 843 purchased new, FCR 202/4/6 from Southampton Corporation and FAD 250 from Cheltenham & District with its second body. CSD 843, a Guy Arab III seen here at Ayr bus station in December 1963, still had its original body new in December 1949. It was, however, replaced by an identical body from FCR 206 in April 1964 and another from FCR 202 a year later, finally being scrapped in 1969. FCR 202 came direct from Southampton. *(JS)*

FCR 206 (and 204), however, came from Graham of Paisley in April 1963, and its body was initially placed on GRH 145 to replace its body damaged in an accident, but it never ran in service. Seen here at Troon, also in December 1963, is FAD 250, an Arab II new in 1943 with a Park Royal body, which was replaced with the one seen here in 1950. It arrived at Troon in 1960 and was withdrawn in December 1965. However, the body appeared on similar CAG 801 (seen earlier) a 1948 Arab III which was withdrawn in May 1966 with upper deck damage. Reappearing in January 1967, CAG 801 had a further accident with this body in June 1969 and was scrapped. *(JS)*

As if this wasn't complicated enough, CAG 800 also new in June 1948, but an Arab II (the last to be built) was also re-bodied, but unlike the others not with another Park Royal body, and is seen here at Ayr bus station with its original body. It was withdrawn in 1965, but re-entered service in March 1967 with a 1955 Massey body from DVD 878 which itself had been re-bodied. It was a Guy Arab II built to Arab III specification new in 1948 to Laurie (Chieftain) of Hamilton with a second-hand body. In October 1961, it passed to Central SMT but was non-standard and withdrawn in 1966. *(RG)*

DVD 878 was sold to Tiger (dealer) Salsburgh, and towed to Troon in April 1966 for spares having acquired a Daimler gearbox and a Leyland rear axle. When CAG 800 reappeared on the road in March 1967 with its Massey H61R body, it also incorporated these features. Despite sustaining severe damage to its roof soon after re-entering service, it was repaired and back on the road again in April 1968. Finally, withdrawn in June 1970, it was sold for scrap. It was photographed at the depot in 1968 beside CU 6311, a Weymann-bodied Arab IV from Northern General, and PUF 631 a Park Royal-bodied Arab IV still in Southdown colours. *(JS)*

When DVD 878 first entered service with Chieftain, it had a 1933 Metro Cammell H52R body first fitted to GS 3918, a Thornycroft Daring of Perth Corporation. After Alexander took over, the body was transferred in 1937 to CP 7574, a 1929 Leyland TD1 acquired from Hebble. This unusual combination was sold in 1945 to Dunlop of Greenock, returning to Millburn Motors two years later. In December 1947, Chieftain bought CP 7574, and after its body was reconditioned by Irvine of Salsburgh, it was fitted to DVD 878. The picture here shows it in service with Chieftain with its Massey body. *(RG)*

Another postwar vehicle to operate in Lanarkshire after being re-bodied by Massey, was an AEC Regal EVJ 807 with Baxter of Airdrie, shown here in the company's two-tone blue livery. It was new in 1947 to Jones of Burley Gate with a Santus C33F body, passing to Hadwin of Ulverston. Acquired by Baxter, it was re-bodied in 1956 with a Massey B35F body, and after Eastern Scottish took over Baxter in December 1962, it was painted into an experimental version of their fleet livery with a green roof. Withdrawn in May 1965, it passed to a showman, still appearing at fairgrounds three years later. *(RG)*

75

Complex re-bodying had been a feature of Western SMT, and Leyland TD3 CS 124 had three bodies during its twenty-seven years. New in June 1934 with a Short H54R body as seen in this picture, it was one of three (CS 124-6) re-bodied in 1945 with utility Alexander lowbridge bodies together with a batch of Leyland TS7s being converted to double-deck specification. Moving to Kilmarnock the following year, they were initially used on the long Ayr to Airdrie service based at Calderbank, an outpost in Lanarkshire from an earlier take-over. Later used on more local services, they continued in daily service until withdrawn in June 1958. *(RG)*

CS 124 is seen here at Kilmarnock depot with its Alexander body before it was sold along with CS 125 and 126 to Millburn Motors in August 1958, where the latter was scrapped. CS 124 and 125 then passed to Northern Roadways where CS 124 was subsequently re-bodied with a probable 1948 postwar Alexander body from a Leyland TD3. Northern Roadways had acquired five TD3s which had been re-bodied thus while operating with Greenock Motor Services, and the recipients of four of these are known. The unidentified donor may be BU 8429, new to Oldham Corporation with a Roe H56R body in 1934 but this is not confirmed. *(RG)*

Western SMT subsidiary Greenock Motor Services (GMS) also bought Short-bodied Leylands, TD3s VS 2603-5 in 1934, and TD4s VS 2720-2 in 1935 and VS 2603 is seen here when new in the red and grey livery. At the end of 1948, they were all fitted with new Alexander L53R bodies to the postwar style, which resembled the final prewar Leyland body. Taken over by Western SMT in November 1949, they initially continued to operate in Greenock, but all ended up on WSMT's outpost on the Isle of Bute. The two batches were withdrawn in 1958 and 1959 passing to Millburn Motors. *(RG)*

VS 2603 was photographed in 1950 on a Greenock town service before receiving any indication of its new ownership. Later, it would receive an illuminated panel above the destination box with 'Local' rather than 'Western' displayed to indicate that it was operating on such a service. Transferred to Rothesay on Bute in 1955, it was withdrawn in July 1958, but saw no further service and was scrapped at Millburn Motors together with the other two TD3s. *(AC)*

VS 2719 was the odd one out. Numerically in the same batch as 2720-2, it arrived two months earlier, and had a 'vee-front' metal-framed Leyland H56R body, although it is believed that the vehicle was ordered with a Short body. This body must have suffered the problems often associated with this era of Leyland body production, because in 1939 it was re-bodied with a Leyland L53R body of current design as seen in this picture, possibly as a warranty measure. However, when VS 2720-2 were sent to Alexander for re-bodying in 1948, it was inexplicably sent too. They all returned still in Greenock Motor Services red and grey colours. *(RG)*

VS 2719 is seen here in 1950 with its third body in thirteen years, on a Greenock local service after passing to Western SMT. It was transferred to Bute in May 1957 and withdrawn in September 1958, also ending up with Northern Roadways in mid-1959. It is unlikely to have operated in service for them, as the body was transferred to BVA 239, a Leyland TD7 new to Central SMT in 1940 with a Leyland L53R body. It had been sold to a dealer in Blackpool in 1956, reaching Northern Roadways via a small Lanarkshire operator Yuille of Larkhall. Such was the complexity of operation of Northern Roadways which was always looking for buses for its large school contract fleet. *(AC)*

Yet more Leylands in the Western SMT fleet were to end up with a third body from the batch of twenty Alexander bodies fitted in 1949 to vehicles in the GMS fleet. WJ 9090 and 9095 were TD3cs new to Sheffield Corporation with Craven H55R bodies which reached WSMT via Alexander and Millburn Motors in 1943. Their chassis were immediately sent to Alexander receiving austerity bodies, and WJ 9090 is seen at Kilmarnock where it operated until withdrawn in 1958. Ending up with Northern Roadways, it received the 1948 Alexander body from BU 8428, one of nine TD3s acquired from Oldham Corporation by GMS. *(RFM)*

CS 5257 also received its third body from this batch, but it was fitted by WSMT in its body shop at Kilmarnock. New as a Leyland TS7 in 1937 with an Alexander C35F body, it was converted to TD4 specification and fitted with an austerity Alexander body in September 1944. Following an accident with a low bridge in June 1958, it surprisingly received the 1948 Alexander body from another of the ex-Oldham TD3s BU 8257 just withdrawn and parked in the yard in Kilmarnock. Photographed inside Ayr depot beside ASD 20/1/3 with their ECW bodies, it was withdrawn after a year, but ran for Service Coaches of Bebside until 1962. *(RG)*

Transferring bodies between chassis was common practice, but the more drastic act of transplanting major body parts was comparatively rare. However Leith of Sanquhar, a long established small operator in a rural village in Dumfriesshire, close to the Ayrshire coal mines, grafted the body of a 1938 Leyland Cheetah to the cab and front bulkhead of a 1949 Crossley. The vehicle concerned was KSM 40, a Crossley SD42/7 new in July 1949 with a Santus C33F body, seen here at their premises in Sanquhar. *(RG)*

The reconstruction was complete in 1962, and KSM 40 was used regularly on the long, desolate route from Lanark down to Sanquhar via Wanlockhead, the highest village in Scotland. I photographed it in 1965 at Sanquhar still operational, but never discovered its fate. The donor vehicle was WG 7508, a Leyland LZ2A new to Alexander in 1938 with an Alexander C39F body, sold to Leith via Millburn Motors in 1957 along with WG 7514. Two years later, similar WG 7620 arrived at Sanquhar and it was also withdrawn in 1962 but by contrast used as the basis for a tow wagon, and its body scrapped. *(JS)*

More orthodox ways of replacing major parts of bodywork after accidents involved fitting new components, inevitably often to a more modern design. This can be seen in this picture taken at Milngavie depot in September 1976 of Leyland Tiger Cubs new in 1961 to Alexander Midland with a unique style of Alexander coach body. RMS 704 shows the "Ford Anglia" appearance, and RMS 707 the standard Alexander rear end in use in January 1976 when it sustained severe damage and was sent back to the coachworks. Surprisingly, it was withdrawn only ten months later and sold to a Glasgow dealer for scrap. *(JS)*

Alexander's coachworks, an independent company since 1949, which had relocated from Stirling to Falkirk in 1958, also produced a unique body style for the batch of ten Albion Nimbuses delivered in 1960 to Alexander with C29F bodies. However, OMS 247 had its ornate front replaced by a simpler contemporary version in 1963 after a serious accident on an extended tour, and was photographed in Glasgow in July 1964. Passing to Highland Omnibuses the following March, it was used on tours and service work until sold in January 1968, finally ending up with a small Ayrshire operator in 1976 for spares. *(JS)*

Dodds of Troon transferred and reconstructed bodies in their workshops, showing imagination and flair. Sometimes however, the vehicles were sent to larger concerns either as a result of major accidents or to modernise their highly regarded coach fleet, particularly when underfloor-engined vehicles began to appear in their fleet in 1951. CCS 781-3 were the last half-cab type of chassis purchased, being Duple-bodied Albion CX39Ns which arrived in February 1949 with full-fronts and 33 seats. Only CCS 781 remained unaltered, continuing until 1960 when sold to a local operator, Holland of Drongan. *(RG)*

CCS 782 sustained severe front and side trim end damage after being stolen, and was sent to Associated Coach Builders, reappearing in July 1954 with a modified front as seen in this picture where it is parked beside LTJ 904, a Foden new in 1950 to Taylor of Leigh with a Bellhouse Hartwell centre-entrance 39-seat body. The chassis of CCS 782 had also been lengthened to accommodate 37 seats. In fact, CCS 783 also underwent this conversion, but by Dodds themselves. As usual with Dodds coaches, both saw further use and CCS 782 was sold to Renfrewshire operator Cunningham of Paisley in 1959, ultimately ending up with Jones of Aberdare in 1962. *(RG)*

Dodds had chosen other chassis and body combinations for its coach purchases after the war, even returning them to different coachbuilders for modernisation. One such batch was of three Burlingham-bodied Bristols (CAG 38-40) in January 1948. With Gardner 6LW engines, these were the first full-sized coaches to appear, and were fitted out luxuriously with 31 seats, later increased to 33. However, by 1958 they were beginning to look dated and a decision was made to have them converted to a contemporary style of full-front. *(RG)*

CAG 38 and 39 were sent to Plaxton in 1958 to be rebuilt to full-front, along with a Plaxton-bodied Foden CAG 802, and were photographed at Troon in May 1964 with CCS 544. It was a Guy Arab III new in 1948 with a Brockhouse DP35F body converted to a breakdown wagon in 1963. CAG 38 was withdrawn after accident damage in September 1964 and dismantled for spares. CAG 39 was withdrawn in May 1967 and sold to a local contractor in Dalry. *(JS)*

83

CAG 40 was the last of the trio of Bristol L6Gs purchased by Dodds in 1948, and is seen here heavily embellished and accessorised for its work in one of Scotland's premier coach fleets. In a more orthodox move, it was returned to Burlingham in 1958 to be rebuilt to full-front, returning with a more contemporary appearance to Burlingham 'Seagull' specification. *(RG)*

However, CAG 40 only remained in the Dodds fleet until April 1963, when it was sold to a small local operator Beigley of Kilbirnie where I photographed it still in Dodds colours in April 1965. It later passed to another small company Edgar of Lochwinnoch, being last licensed in September 1967. *(JS)*

Despite having bought two new Burlingham-bodied AEC Regal IVs in 1951, Dodds continued to source modernised half-cab vehicles. Having a penchant for Guys, in 1952 they acquired two Guy Arab IIIs (DTY 789/90) new to Armstrong of Westerhope in 1949 with rare Gurney Nutting C33F bodies and Meadows engines. Both were rebuilt by Dodds to full-front, but each to a different design, and DTY 790 was photographed at Ayr bus station. As was customary, both were sold on to local Ayrshire operators when they appeared outdated, 789 to McNair of Girvan in 1961 who ran it for another seven years, and 790 to Kennedy of Maybole in 1960 where it only survived for a couple of years. *(RG)*

An even more exotic purchase for the Dodds coach fleet in 1954 was EKV 930, a Guy Arab I new to Coventry Corporation in 1943 with a Brush L55R body. The chassis alone passed to a dealer in Brixton in October 1952 and on to Dodds six months later. In the Troon workshops, the chassis was lengthened, fitted with a Meadows engine and sent to Associated Coach Builders in December 1953 who mounted this futuristic 37-seat body. Not withdrawn until 1965, it had a somewhat ignominious end with the General School of Motoring in Glasgow. *(RG)*

As well as building rigid car transporters and constructing new bus bodies, McLennan also rebuilt and modernised buses it acquired for its own fleet or for selling on. Such a vehicle was HUF 290, a Leyland PS1 new to Southdown Motor services in 1949 with a Beadle C32R body, which was itself modernised by Beadle in 1954, by converting it to full-front. Withdrawn in 1959, it passed to Rennie of Cairneyhill in Fife and to McLennan in June 1963. Before entering service, it was converted to C35F to permit OMO operation, and was photographed at Dunkeld in 1965 on service from Spittalfield. *(JS)*

Another half-cab single-decker to be rebuilt and converted to full-front by the original bodybuilder was RC 9693, an AEC Regal new to Trent Motor Traction in 1947 with a Willowbrook B35F body. In July 1958, with the chassis extended to 30 feet, Willowbrook rebuilt the body to FDP39F as seen in this photograph taken at Sanquhar in July 1965, Leith having acquired it in September 1963. Parked beside it are DRN 280, an ex-Ribble Motor Services PD2 with a Leyland L53R body and platform doors, and HD 7887, an ex-Yorkshire Woollen District PS1 with a Brush B34F body acquired from AA member Young. *(JS)*

86

The larger companies tended to rely less on attempts to modernise individual buses because of their ability to purchase larger fleets of new coaches, but Alexander surprisingly chose two 1949 Daimler half-cabs to be converted to full-front. BWG 571 and 573 were members of a second batch of five CVD6s new with Burlingham C33F bodies which in 1953 were still confined to coach duties. Of the first batch of thirty, seven were sold after a year, the remainder of those with Midland being withdrawn in 1965 as seen in this line-up at its headquarters at Larbert Road in August of that year. *(JS)*

After the division of the Alexander empire into separate Midland, Fife and Northern companies in 1961, four Daimlers from the first batch came to Northern. Two retained the coach livery and the two at Elgin, BMS 405 and 407 seen here at the depot in September 1964, were painted into the bus version of the new livery and lasted until 1970. Parked behind it is ASF 378 one of the four ex-SMT TS7s with Alexander B35R bodies replaced with Duple C33F bodies in 1951 and the only one to be painted into fleet colours. It was withdrawn in 1964 and sold for scrap. *(JS)*

While the two Daimlers could have been sent back to Burlingham to have full-fronts fitted, they were in fact sent down to Eastern Coach Works in 1953 so that they would present a uniform appearance to the casual observer, as the company had received 13 CVD6s in 1951 with 'Queen Mary' ECW C37F bodies which were still used as front line coaches. They were, however, withdrawn at the same time as the non-converted vehicles, BWG 571 passing to a Glasgow contractor and 573 sold for scrap. The latter was photographed leaving its home depot of Kilsyth early one cold morning in December 1964 to take up a private hire. *(JS)*

A previous attempt to modernise Burlingham-bodied coaches took place in 1952, when nine of the remaining twenty Leyland Cheetahs new in 1938 with Burlingham C35F bodies were fitted with full-fronts, the work being completed at the company workshops at Kirkcaldy. They had all been fitted with AEC engines after the war, and survived until 1961 or 1962, six having passed to Fife. One of these I photographed at St Andrews in 1956 parked at the depot beside a 1953 Leyland Royal Tiger with an Alexander 'Coronation Coach' body which makes an interesting comparison. WG 7260 was still a front line coach at Kelty depot then, despite being eighteen years old. Withdrawn in 1962, it passed to a showman. *(JS)*

88

Apart from an early order for AEC Regals in 1947, the preferred vehicle for MacBrayne's long distance services after the war was the Park Royal-bodied Maudslay Marathon. Thirty were purchased between 1947 and 1949, the body design being similar to that used on prewar AEC Regals. With high-back seats and luxury internal features, they had considerable appeal, but were beginning to look dated by the late nineteen fifties. Most were sent to Bennet, a Glasgow coachbuilder, who rebuilt the bodies, reglazing the windows and GUS 409 parked at Fort William bus station in 1962 shows evidence of this. *(JS)*

While four of these Maudslays received new Duple bodies, rather surprisingly three which underwent refurbishment in Bennet's coach works in 1958 also received full-fronts. However, one was sold to a Renfrewshire operator within four years. GUS 411 was photographed parked at the same location in 1964, and has been thus modernised and in a later version of the livery with less cream. All three, however, continued on local and short distance services in the Fort William area, GUS 411 due to leave for the nearby village of Inverlochy. The last of the trio to be withdrawn, it was scrapped in March 1965. *(JS)*

89

Among the very earliest postwar single-deck bodies built by Alexander, were twenty-five metal-framed C35F bodies for SMT (FFS 182-206), none of which required replacement, most surviving until 1964/5 and many seeing further service thereafter. FFS 197 was such a vehicle, new in April 1947, passing to a local contractor seventeen years later. It was photographed at Edinburgh bus station in March 1964, displaying an incorrect registration mark, six months before withdrawal. Parked beside it is JGD 978, a 1951 AEC Regal IV with a Burlingham C35C body new to Lowland Motors, passing to SMT in 1958. Surprisingly, it was scrapped two years after this picture. *(JS)*

The 1948 batch of AEC Regals (FFS 207-41), however, all had composite bodies, which did require replacement, either with Burlingham Seagull bodies (FFS207-26) or essentially new bodies with full-fronts (FFS 227-41). The last ten vehicles to leave Alexanders only had 30 coach seats, although capacities did change in relation to their use on the premium Edinburgh to London service. Photographed at the terminus are two of the coaches delivered with 30 seats, FFS 220 and 229 new in June 1948 and both re-bodied within five years. The fate of these particular two bodies is not known. *(AC)*

The final 15 of these Alexander-bodied AEC Regals reappeared in 1953 with bodies purported to have been rebuilt by Dickinson of Dunbar. However, there is considerable doubt about the whole exercise, and to what extent SMT's own workshops at Marine Gardens had contributed to the finished product. In the event, they emerged with chassis extended to 30ft, an 8ft wide body with a full-front, and some features similar to the bodies SMT was building on former London Transport Guy Arabs. FFS 229 was photographed at Edinburgh bus station in 1962, being withdrawn the following year and passing to a contractor in Scunthorpe. *(JS)*

Classified as dual-purpose vehicles with 35 high-back seats they carried out a wide variety of duties, and FFS 233 is seen at the bus stances in Edinburgh about to depart on an excursion. Initially allocated to Edinburgh with the rest of the batch, all but one were eventually dispersed around other depots. FFS 233 was transferred to the borders depot at Galashiels in 1961, and withdrawn in 1962 with the rest of the batch. With bodies that were effectively only nine years old, all found further operators, apart from two that were not traced, and FFS 233 ended up with a ski club in Fife. *(RG)*

The twenty vehicles from the 1948 intake of AEC Regals which received new Burlingham Seagull bodies in 1953 fared little better, as all were gone by 1965. They too followed the same pattern of being cascaded down to peripheral depots, but FFS 212, photographed at Edinburgh bus station just before withdrawal in April 1965, had returned to its home depot for the final few months as often happened, and was on a Saturday only single journey to a village in the Scottish Borders. It was sold to the contractor Cruden of Musselburgh with five others of this batch, and eleven more going to other contractors. Only three of this batch were unaccounted for after being sold to local dealer Locke. *(JS)*

During the 1960s, Locke was the preferred dealer for Scottish Omnibuses disposals, including double-deckers, and many were sold to local contractor Cruden. Seen in this representative line-up at Musselburgh in March 1968 are AEC Regals FFS 223 and GSF 715 re-bodied with Burlingham Seagull bodies and FFS 240 re-bodied with a full-front body nominally by Dickinson of Dunbar. Also in the line-up is HWS 913 from the batch of twenty-six 'London' coaches with 30-seat Alexander bodies with toilets on AEC Regal IV chassis. These remained essentially unaltered apart from frontal modification until withdrawn in 1963, or 1966 as was HWS 913. *(JS)*

Lesser modifications were carried out to vehicle fronts after major accidents, often altering the appearance considerably, but without complete replacement. Often grilles were replaced or modified, as seen below with Eastern Scottish AEC Reliance OVD 108 new to Baxter of Airdrie in June 1957 with a Burlingham DP45F body passing to Eastern Scottish in December 1962. By comparison, identical UVA 116 is shown photographed in Baxter livery at the depot in June 1964, although it was later to appear in both Eastern Scottish livery in August 1967 and Starks colours in May 1972 being withdrawn in March 1973. *(JS)*

Seven of the eight AEC Reliances with Burlingham DP45F bodies were transferred from the Baxter operation to the Eastern Scottish depot in Edinburgh at different times, OVD 108 moving in October 1967. Following an accident, it reappeared with its modified front in June 1968, and was photographed at Edinburgh bus station in May 1969. Withdrawn in 1970, it was initially used for decimal currency training, and later sold to Locke in October 1971, passing to Dodds of Troon for spares, and ultimately to a dealer in Coatbridge for scrap. *(JS)*

Another vehicle acquired from an Independent by a Scottish Bus Group company to receive major modification to its front was Leyland Tiger Cub WVA 809, new to Carmichael of Glenboig in 1960 with a Duple Midland C41F body. Passing to Alexander Midland in August 1966, it continued as a front line coach at Cumbernauld depot which housed the former Carmichael fleet, until withdrawn in June 1975. After an accident in December 1969, it reappeared with a modified front, only to experience a fire the following August, but was subsequently repaired again. However, I had caught it on camera in June 1971 in Glasgow on a private hire with its new grille. *(JS)*

Another vehicle to experience two major accidents in its lifetime (a not uncommon situation), in this case on the same service from Oban to Glasgow on which the vehicle operated regularly for two years, was Highland Omnibuses Albion Viking FGM 103D. One of a batch of five new to Central SMT in their blue coach livery in May 1966 with Alexander C40F bodies, it moved north in June 1967. It was photographed at the workshops in Inverness in June 1971 after its second accident beside FGM 104D, allowing comparison of their fronts and liveries, FGM 103D having just been painted into the new poppy red and peacock blue colours. *(JS)*

A more bulbous front was fitted to a Leyland Royal Tiger (DWG 692) in the Alexander Fife fleet in early 1968. Alexander had acquired a batch of standard Leyland-bodied Leyland Royal Tigers with C41C bodies, ordered by a haulage contractor, George Rodger of Motherwell, who had intended to introduce express services from Scotland. They entered service in 1952 amidst the first batch of Royal Tigers with Alexander 'Coronation Coach' bodies, with five allocated to the Northern area and five to Fife. DWG 692 was allocated to Kirkcaldy depot in Fife, and was photographed in 1964 on Kirkcaldy esplanade. *(JS)*

DWG 692 was painted into Fife's coach colours when the Alexander empire was split up in 1961, and continued as a front line coach at Kirkcaldy until transferred to the nearby industrial town of Cowdenbeath in August 1965, where it was principally used on contract work. After its accident in 1968, the front was rebuilt in the coachworks at Kirkcaldy, and it returned to Cowdenbeath where I photographed it in July 1968, parked beside the last Guy Arab from the Alexander fleet to remain in service. It was withdrawn in 1970, passing to a dealer in Preston in September. *(JS)*

Fife was introducing OMO operation to its rural depots in the late nineteen sixties, but still had eleven centre-entrance Royal Tigers in service. However, Leyland bodied DWG 525 had a major accident in July 1965, and was fitted with a new contemporary Alexander front, moving the entrance forwards. It returned to service in October, now allocated to the small rural depot at Cupar where I photographed it in July 1967 now repainted into all red service bus livery and fitted for OMO operation. It too was withdrawn in 1970, and sold to Telefilms of Preston. *(JS)*

One other Fife Leyland-bodied Royal Tiger (DWG 694) was also similarly converted, but differing in detail as can be seen in these pictures. There was no clear history of an accident, and the conversion to C41F appears to have taken place early in 1966. It too returned to service in the all cream coach livery, and was photographed at Aberhill depot in July 1968, although it was actually allocated to a smaller depot in the fishing village of Anstruther. By December 1969, it had a red roof but was never painted into the all red livery. Withdrawn at the end of 1970, it was scrapped by local dealer Muir at Kirkcaldy. *(JS)*

Three of Fife's six Alexander-bodied Royal Tigers were converted to C41F, although it is believed none were ever operated OMO. The first was EMS 168 in May 1965 which was painted in the all cream coach livery, and reallocated to St Andrews depot. It was photographed in Glasgow on a newly introduced but short lived St Andrews to Glasgow express service, but repainted into all red bus livery a year later and transferred to the main depot at Kirkcaldy. Two others, EMS 170/1, were converted later in the year, but repainted straight into bus livery and used on normal service work. All were withdrawn in 1970. *(JS)*

Northern acquired 16 Leyland Royal Tigers, of which eleven had Alexander bodies, but only three of these were ever converted to C41F. All retained their coach livery, and none were operated OMO. The Leyland-bodied vehicles were also repainted into coach colours and remained unaltered, being withdrawn in 1972 with nine of the Alexander-bodied vehicles. BMS 222 (numerically the first of Alexander's eighty-four PC class) photographed at Aberdeen bus station in 1968 was converted in early 1967 together with EMS 511, but has reverted back to C41C specification in preservation. The last to appear was EMS 512 in July 1968. *(JS)*

More unusual vehicles to appear in Aberdeen with body conversions to front entrance were a pair of Aberdeen Corporation's Daimler CVD6s (CRG 809 and 811), new in 1947 with locally built Walker B34R bodies. Both were rebuilt to front entrance in 1956 as B31F and converted to OMO operation with five similar vehicles. While the remainder were extensively refurbished in 1962 as C31F, these two had received the last half-cab bodies built by Alexander, in June 1958. CRG 811 was photographed at the depot with its C35F body, and this rear view shows the resemblance to current Alexander products of that time. *(JS)*

CRG 809 had been withdrawn in 1971 passing to Alexander (Greyhound) of Arbroath, but CRG 811 was not sold until January 1972, also moving south to McLennan of Spittalfield where it is seen parked beside another former Aberdeen Corporation bus which has been re-bodied, Daimler CVG6 DRS 365. Entering service in March, fully converted for OMO operation with a cut-away cab, it was withdrawn in 1975 eventually entering preservation, and is currently stored with the Glasgow Vintage Vehicle Trust at Bridgeton. *(RG)*

McLennan acquired a remarkable collection of vehicles over many years, most rebuilt or modified at sometime in the body shops at Spittalfield, in addition to constructing completely new bodies. Such a vehicle was GDK 301, a Leyland PS1 new to Yelloway Motor Services in June 1948 with a Trans-United C33F body, acquired in April 1958 and converted for OMO operation. GDK 303 arrived a year later and was similarly treated. GDK 301 was photographed at Errol parked beside ex-London Transport RTL47 (JXN 370) on service from Perth, before sale the following year to Duncan of Kinloch Rannoch. *(RG)*

GDK 301 returned to McLennan in February 1963, and was fitted with the last new body built by the company, being constructed for OMO operation with a cut-away cab and 36 seats. It was the regular vehicle on the Errol to Dundee service, being outstationed at their three-vehicle depot at Errol and was photographed at the Dundee terminus of the service in October 1965 parked beside Dundee Corporation's CTS 633 a Weymann-bodied Daimler CVD6. Only GDK 301 was re-bodied, and GDK 303 and GDK 9-10 Leyland PS1s with Burlingham bodies which were also purchased, ran for McLennan with their original bodies, albeit converted for OMO operation. *(JS)*

During the refurbishment of acquired vehicles, not only did McLennan convert many single-deckers for OMO operation, but double-deckers were frequently fitted with platform doors. Such a vehicle was DRS 368, one of five Daimler CVG6s new to Aberdeen Corporation in 1951 with Northern Coachbuilders bodies and re-bodied by Alexander in 1960, which ended up with McLennan. It was photographed at their depot at Stanley in August 1972 beside STJ 989. This was a Leyland Tiger Cub new in 1954 to Walls of Higher Ince with an Alexander C41F body, acquired in 1961 and now fitted with bus seats, which ran until 1979. *(JS)*

McLennan had fitted platform doors to most double-deckers it acquired, usually before entering service, including the entire batch of eleven Leyland TD6cs they obtained from Birmingham City Transport in 1950. New in 1939 they had Metro-Cammell H52R bodies to 'Birmingham' design. They also had their torque converters replaced with four-speed crash gearboxes, and gave long service with McLennan. EOG 277 was photographed leaving Perth, showing the neatly fitted platform door. It was withdrawn as early as November 1958, but the last of the batch was not withdrawn until six years later after twenty-five years use with its original body. *(RG)*

Another company to purchase TD6s from Birmingham was Laurie (Chieftain) of Hamilton who bought nine in 1952/3. One of these passed to Central SMT in 1961, although it was never repainted and never carried its fleet number (HL185). EOG 215 had a complex history, as it was bombed in 1942 with eleven others of its contemporaries, and was given a new English Electric H54R body which had been built for a Manchester Corporation Daimler COG5, hence its 'Mancunian' appearance. A Chieftain variant of a 'tin front' had been fitted to modernise it further. Ironically, in the background is FOF 187 an ex-Birmingham Daimler COG5 with a Metro-Cammell H54R body. *(RG)*

Another re-bodied vehicle in the Chieftain fleet whose body had been embellished in the coach works at Hamilton was EAX 641. It was an Albion CX13 new to Red and White Services of Chepstow, one of a batch of twelve delivered in 1941 with Duple L56R bodies. Briefly operated by Bristol Tramways, it returned to Red and White in 1951 when it was re-bodied with a further Duple body. Chieftain bought it in 1955, designed and fitted the full-front and added platform doors, and ran it until 1959 when it was sold to nearby operator Nolan of Motherwell. *(RG)*

An unusual conversion was that of ex-London Transport RTL 43 to front entrance. T&E Docherty of Irvine bought it from the dealer Bird of Stratford in March 1958 when ten years old, and it joined AI Motor Services fleet of Craven-bodied RTs and Park Royal-bodied RTLs. However, it went into the workshops of a local Ayrshire coachbuilder, reappearing in September 1963 as H32/25FD. It was photographed in August 1964 leaving Kilmarnock bus station on the high frequency service to Ardrossan, which retained conductors long after OMO had been widely introduced, but JXN 366 was never considered for this. *(JS)*

In June 1968, JXN 366 was photographed at Ardrossan bus station parked behind EAG 10, a Leyland PD2 new in 1950 with a Leyland H56R body. In April 1971 it passed to another AI operator, JM Duff of Ardrossan. It was delicensed in early 1973, put back on the road again in July, and sold to dealer Tiger Coaches of Salsburgh in November, then passing into preservation. Whether regarded as a possible forerunner for further conversions, it remained unique, and Docherty's other Leyland RTL LYF 118 remained unaltered. *(JS)*

A more radical transformation took place with Edinburgh Corporation's unique Leyland Leopard YSG 101, exhibited at the 1961 Scottish Motor Show with a rear entrance and front and centre exits. It entered service in April 1962, and as a student, I tried to time my journey home in order to travel on it, although I did not realise it only ever was a duplicate when operating the 16 service from Oxgangs to Silverknowes, on which it was photographed in October 1961 at Greenbank Church in Morningside. *(JS)*

In May 1969, it was converted to front entrance, and fitted with 45 dual-purpose seats for the Edinburgh Airport service, appearing in the black and white coach livery, and was photographed in July at St Andrews Square leaving for the airport. However, it was repainted back into madder and white in March 1975, and reverted to service work on routes requiring OMO operation, eventually entering preservation. *(JS)*

Accidental decapitation is rare, sometimes only requiring a replacement roof before return to service. Strathclyde PTE Ailsa B55-10 MGE 185P, new in 1975 with an Alexander H78F body, reappeared as a 38-seat single-decker after an accident in May 1985. However, the paperwork was incomplete, and when sold to Black Prince of Morley, it did not enter service and was cannibalised. Returning to service in coach livery, it was unusually operating a tendered service from Larkfield depot to the Stirlingshire village of Balfron, (where First still have an allocation of nineteen buses) an hour from the city boundary, when photographed in 1988 near Croftamie. *(JS)*

By contrast, Strathclyde converted eight of its panoramic window Alexander-bodied Atlanteans to single-deck configuration initially for use on the inter-station service 98 between Central Station and Queen Street station where JUS 777N (SA2) was photographed in August 1982 shortly after entering service. It had arrived new in June 1975 with an Alexander H76F body. The batch was used on a variety of shuttle and outer suburb services, but also sent to small operators throughout Strathclyde Region, and JUS 777N was sent to the Isle of Cumbrae to help Millport Motors between July 1983 and January 1984. Withdrawn in November 1988, it went to a Barnsley dealer for scrap. *(JS)*

104

A further double-decker converted after an accident, which ran in Glasgow, was Daimler Fleetline TWH 697T. It actually operated for four companies, Greens of Kirkintilloch, Morrow of Clydebank and Kelvin Central Buses, finally passing to local City Sightseeing operator Scotguide who operated it for a couple of weeks before it was withdrawn for spares. It is seen here at Greens depot in June 1991, but passed to Morrow of Clydebank when Kelvin Central Buses acquired Greens. However, Morrow was taken over by Kelvin Central Buses in August 1992, and TWH 697T joined the fleet, operating on a variety of routes until passing to Alex Pringle's Sightseeing operation in 1995. *(JS)*

TWH 697T was new to Lancashire United in August 1978 with a Northern Counties H75F body. In 1985 with Greater Manchester PTE, following an accident under Wargrave Railway Bridge near Newton-le Willows, it was sent back to Northern Counties to be converted to a single-decker. It was then allocated to Bury depot for a service to Holcome Brook which required such a vehicle. With Kelvin Central Buses, it operated on a variety of routes, but was photographed in November 1992, still in a preliminary Kelvin livery, on a rural service passing Lennox Castle Hospital en route from Blanefield to Kirkintilloch. *(JS)*

A more limited reconstruction was required when two of WSMT's 49-seat Leopards with Alexander bodies sustained severe rear end damage in 1979, and emerged from their workshops in November 1979 (YSD 365L) and March 1980 (YSD 350L) as B41F being required for a new local service in Erskine for which a small bus was necessary. Pictured here is YSD 365L at the Bargarran terminus of the route. They subsequently moved to rural depots at Stranraer and Dumfries in 1983 and 1984, and transferred to Northern in January 1987, returning to WSMT in 1988 for a further four years. *(JS)*

The conversion of 45-seat Plaxton Derwent Ford R192 YHA 390J to a B27F midibus was, however, a company decision. New to Midland Red in March 1971, it was delicensed in March 1978 to have the work carried out, returning in June, but withdrawn as soon as October 1980. It passed to McLeod of Dunvegan in Skye in January 1981 for a school contract from the remote community of Geary near Waternish Point along single track roads to Dunvegan Primary School. I photographed it at Dunvegan in 1983, where it was parked up for the school holidays. *(JS)*

More unusual conversions involved fitting mail compartments to buses, and one of the most elegant was carried out to Highland Omnibuses Ford R1114 OST 261S at their Inverness body shop in September 1981. New in 1977 with a standard Alexander B53F body, it now had 31 seats and was required for a mail service from Tongue to Thurso which also carried items for local hotels. Its predecessor was a Bedford VAM (CST 961D) new in 1966 with an Alexander B24F body built for this purpose, and the replacement took place on 19th October 1981 when I photographed the changeover at Ardgay as OST 261S went north and the Bedford headed south to Inverness. Surprisingly, it was withdrawn for scrap five years later and not replaced. *(JS)*

A spare vehicle had been required for this contract, and two five-year-old Bedford VAS with Duple DP28F bodies were altered in 1969 to accommodate a small mail compartment and 19 seats. The conversion, however, was temporary as WST 500, seen here in August 1971 at Portree on Skye when on loan, had the compartment removed two years later and reseated with 27 bus seats from a withdrawn 'ski bus', ECK 584. However, these were replaced five years later with DP seats again, and the vehicle withdrawn in 1977 having seen little service since 1971. Nevertheless, its remains still exist to this day on Orkney. *(JS)*

A more imaginative conversion was carried out to six Leyland Royal Tigers obtained by Highland Omnibuses from Ribble Motor Services via Millburn Motors in Preston in 1967. They were new in 1952 with Leyland B44F bodies, and initially ran as purchased. However, Highland had just acquired Smith of Grantown who operated services to the ski grounds on Cairngorm, and required suitable vehicles for transporting passengers with skis. This picture shows a line-up at the Highland Omnibuses depot at Grantown on Spey station in July 1968 with ECK 604 in the 'new' livery. Despite having destination boxes, paper stickers were routinely used. *(JS)*

The conversion work was carried out by Alexander in their body shops at Falkirk, and they returned one by one with a uniquely created rear platform for skis and 38 seats. However, the logistics of operating a network of rural services required them to be used on school and shoppers services as they were converted for OMO operation, and ECK 588 was photographed near the village of Kincraig. They had a surprisingly short life, despite the substantial work carried out on them, and they were all withdrawn by November 1971 and inevitably scrapped, although one did survive as a company seat store for two years. *(JS)*

A different form of transformation took place with ex-London Transport Guy Arab GYL 402 whose chassis was acquired by Western SMT and fitted with a Northern Counties L55R body in August 1954 reregistered to FSD 458. Delicensed as early as March 1966, it moved to Highland Omnibuses in July 1967 and was photographed at Inverness in October beside ECK 599 still to be converted to a 'ski bus.' FSD 458 was never repainted into Highland colours, but allocated to the fishing village of Helmsdale on the east coast of Sutherland for a school service down to Golspie. Withdrawn a year later, it was sent for scrap. *(JS)*

Ten former London Transport utility Guys were involved in the re-bodying exercise, the chassis going direct to Wigan to have their new bodies fitted before reaching the WSMT headquarters at Kilmarnock. As FSD 454-63, they were all initially allocated to Johnstone depot, and FSD 462 was photographed at its sub-depot in Paisley in December 1965 parked beside ESD 217 a Guy Arab III new in 1953 with a similar body. All ten were withdrawn in 1967 as was ESD 217, with FSD 462 being sold for scrap. FSD 459 passed to Fife in August 1966 initially on loan, but was never repainted either and also withdrawn for scrap in February 1968. *(JS)*

Dodds of Troon operated many rebuilt and re-bodied utility Guys, but two disguised their origin being reregistered because of the modification required before new bodies were fitted. KAG 574 started off life as Plymouth Corporation Arab II CDR 673, new in 1943 with a Roe L55R body. Acquired in 1954, it was not operated but was fitted with a Gardner 6LW engine and Mark III radiator, entering service with an Alexander H63RD body in April 1957. It was photographed at Ayr bus station beside similar KAG 575, a Leyland PD2/20 of fellow AA operator Young and Guy Arab II, DGG 910, re-bodied with a Roe B38C body. *(JS)*

A further ex-Plymouth Corporation Guy Arab II with a Gardner 5LW engine, CDR 757, had the same chassis preparation carried out at Troon, but did not reappear until June 1960 as OSD 178 when it returned from Wigan with a Northern Counties FH37/27F body later reduced to 34 seats upstairs because of the instability of an 8' wide body on a 7'6" chassis. It lasted three years longer than KAG 574, being withdrawn in February 1973 and sold for scrap. Parked beside it at Ayr bus station are KAG 574 and OCS 901, a Leyland PD3 belonging to Young with a Northern Counties H39/30F body also new in 1960. *(JS)*

One of the most unexpected re-bodying exercises occurred when Western SMT had to replace the Strachan bodies on its fifteen Leyland PD1s within three years. Of light alloy construction, they had started to disintegrate, and were dispatched to Lowestoft for new bodies. The first six had been delivered to subsidiary Greenock Motor Services in 1948, and VS 4867 is seen before entry into service. They all passed to Western SMT in November 1949, and after returning with Eastern Coachworks bodies at the beginning of 1953, were soon reallocated to WSMT depots, being withdrawn at the end of 1966. *(RG)*

VS 4867 was reallocated, eventually reaching Newton Mearns depot in May 1955 where in a large allocation of PD1s, it was employed on intensive services from Glasgow to peripheral Renfrewshire suburbs. Photographed on a day of sleet and rain in January 1965, this poor picture shows it lined up with a couple of re-bodied PD1s from WSMT's own allocation (CCS 403-11) and a Leyland bodied PD1 from the twenty-five delivered to the depot in 1947. Of the six PD1s new to GMS, all were scrapped, apart from one which went to Northern Roadways. Many of the Leyland-bodied PD1s, however, saw further use with a variety of operators. *(JS)*

111

Western SMT's nine Strachan-bodied PD1s all operated from Newton Mearns depot on their flagship route from Glasgow down to the popular holiday resort of Ayr, and continued to do so with their ECW bodies until 1955/6 when superseded by new Leyland PD2/20s. CCS 410 is seen here in Ayr passing ASD 95, a 1943 Guy Arab I with a Gardner 5LW engine and a Massey H56R body which spent its entire fourteen year life on Ayr town services. While the body of ASD 94 was beyond economic repair, that on ASD 95 had major reconstruction carried out in their workshops in December 1949, using Leyland/Alexander parts as seen here. *(RG)*

Apart from the body of CCS 406 being fitted to PD2/20 GCS 232, and CCS 404 passing to Northern Roadways, the remainder of the batch were scrapped with one exception. CCS 407 had been on loan to Fife from August 1966 (with Guy Arab FSD 459), and remained there when the rest of the batch were withdrawn. Allocated to Lochgelly depot, which provided services to the Fife coalfields, it was photographed there in Fife colours in April 1967 with the fleet number FRB163 suggesting it was a PD2, rather than the correct FRA prefix. It continued at Lochgelly until withdrawn after an accident in December 1969, and was sent for scrap the following May. *(JS)*